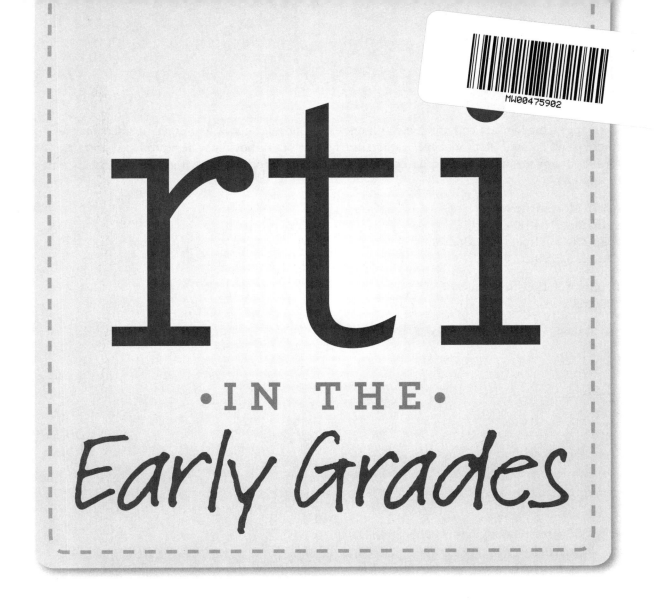

rti

• IN THE •

Early Grades

Intervention Strategies for
Mathematics, Literacy, Behavior &
Fine-Motor Challenges

CHRIS WEBER

Solution Tree | Press

a division of

Solution Tree

555 North Morton Street
Bloomington, IN 47404
800.733.6786 (toll free) / 812.336.7700
FAX: 812.336.7790

email: info@solution-tree.com
solution-tree.com

Printed in the United States of America

16 15 14 13 12   1 2 3 4 5

Library of Congress Cataloging-in-Publication Data
Weber, Chris, 1948-
  RTI in the early grades : intervention strategies for mathematics, literacy, behavior, and fine-motor challenges / Chris Weber.
      pages cm
  Includes bibliographical references and index.
  ISBN 978-1-936764-04-4 (perfect bound) 1. Remedial teaching. 2. Response to intervention (Learning disabled children) 3. Learning disabled children--Education--United States. 4. Education, Elementary--United States. I. Title.
  LB1029.R4W44 2013
  371.9--dc23
  2012035697

Solution Tree
Jeffrey C. Jones, CEO
Edmund M. Ackerman, President

Solution Tree Press
President: Douglas M. Rife
Publisher: Robert D. Clouse
Editorial Director: Lesley Bolton
Managing Production Editor: Caroline Wise
Senior Production Editor: Suzanne Kraszewski
Proofreader: Rachel Rosolina
Cover and Text Designer: Jenn Taylor

For Rebecca

ACKNOWLEDGMENTS

I have been blessed to have the most phenomenal professional mentors, including but not limited to Leslie Fausset, Harry Weinberg, Sherine Smith, Austin Buffum, and Joey Wise. Among my most gifted and cherished mentors is Laura Schwalm. The district she has led for well over a decade and in which she has served for nearly four decades is simply one of the best school districts in the country; Garden Grove Unified School District in California won the 2004 Broad Prize for Urban Education and is a phenomenal organization that does things the right way—with success! Students learn at high levels, and no one is ever satisfied. My brief tenure serving with and learning from Laura Schwalm provided the inspiration for so much in this book. I would also like to express my gratitude to Si Swun for his friendship and service to students through Swun Math.

Solution Tree has been amazingly good to me and, more importantly, to educators and subsequently to students around the world. Thanks to Jeff Jones, Ed Ackerman, Douglas Rife, Robb Clouse, Shannon Ritz, Gretchen Knapp, Claudia Wheatley, Kelly Rockhill, Caroline Wise, and Suzanne Kraszewski.

Solution Tree Press would like to thank the following reviewers:

Thomasenia Lott Adams
Professor
School of Teaching & Learning
University of Florida
Gainesville, Florida

Tanya Anastasia
Kindergarten Teacher
Mountain Brook Elementary School
Mountain Brook, Alabama

Marcia Birk
Principal
Central School Road Early Childhood
  Center
St. Charles, Missouri

Beth Kobett McCord
Assistant Professor
Stevenson University
Stevenson, Maryland

Cathie West
Principal
Mountain Way Elementary School
Granite Falls, Washington

Marilyn Grady
Professor of Educational Administration
University of Nebraska
Lincoln, Nebraska

Becky Newman-Gonchar
Senior Research Associate
Instructional Research Group
Los Alamitos, California

Jennifer Bonicelli
Intervention Coordinator/SAL
Westerly Creek Elementary
Denver Public Schools
Denver, Colorado

Linda Hitchings
Literacy Coach
University Elementary School
Bloomington, Indiana

Shelly Zimbro
Instructional Supervisor
Federal Programs
Newport News, Virginia

TABLE OF CONTENTS

Reproducible pages are in italics.

ABOUT THE AUTHOR

 **CHRIS WEBER, EDD,** works in Distinctive Schools in the city of Chicago and consults with schools and school districts across the United States and Canada.

As principal of R. H. Dana Elementary School in the Capistrano Unified School District (CUSD) in California, Chris was the leader of a highly effective professional learning community. Together with his staff, they lifted the school to remarkable levels of success. Designated Schoolwide Title I, with more than 60 percent of all students English learners and Latino and more than 75 percent socioeconomically disadvantaged, R. H. Dana consistently exceeded adequate yearly progress (AYP) goals. The school's gains over four years were among the top 1 percent in the state, and it was the first school in the decades-long history of the CUSD to win the State of California's Title I Academic Achievement Award. Under Chris's leadership, R. H. Dana earned the first California Distinguished School Award in the school's forty-two-year history. After the percentage of students meeting AYP in English and math quadrupled in four years, the school was named a National Blue Ribbon School. Chris credits these achievements to staff and stakeholders embracing the premises of the PLC model and response to intervention.

Chris has experience teaching grades K–12 and has served as a site administrator for elementary and secondary schools. He was director of instruction for the Garden Grove Unified School District in California, which was the 2004 winner of the prestigious Broad Prize for Urban Education. Chris led the district's forty-seven K–6 schools in helping all groups of students achieve double-digit AYP gains in mathematics and English language arts.

Chris is a coauthor of *Pyramid Response to Intervention: RTI, Professional Learning Communities, and How to Respond When Kids Don't Learn, Pyramid of Behavior Interventions: Seven Keys to a Positive Learning Environment*, and *Simplifying Response to Intervention: Four Essential Guiding Principles*. He also coauthored "The Why Behind RTI," the feature article in the October 2010 issue of *Educational Leadership*.

A graduate of the United States Air Force Academy and a former U.S. Air Force pilot, he holds a master's degree from California State University, San Marcos, and a doctorate of education from the University of California (Irvine and Los Angeles).

Follow Chris on Twitter @Chi_educate.

To book Chris for professional development, contact pd@solution-tree.com.

INTRODUCTION

*We can succeed only by concert. It is not "can any of us
imagine better?" but, "can we all do better?" The dogmas
of the quiet past are inadequate to the stormy present.
The occasion is piled high with difficulty, and we must rise
with the occasion. As our case is new, so we must
think anew, and act anew.*

ABRAHAM LINCOLN

We can predict that despite our best efforts, some students will experience difficulties during their schooling and will require additional supports. Many educators, schools, and school systems have embraced response to intervention (RTI) as a method for providing such support. This approach includes three parts (Buffum, Mattos, & Weber, 2009, 2012):

1. Rigorous, differentiated Tier 1 (core) instruction for all students so that fewer and fewer interventions are necessary

2. Preventative, proactive steps on behalf of students based on predictable roadblocks to learning and progress

3. A well-designed, comprehensive system of supports for all students

In some schools, however, RTI is little more than reactive, one-size-fits-all Tier 2 and Tier 3 interventions for students who are perpetually underserved by core instruction. Moreover, efforts at leveraging the power and potential of RTI have been shaped by the pressures of No Child Left Behind (NCLB, 2002) and adequate yearly progress (AYP). While some schools have established supports that meet the needs of all students—students with the lowest readiness levels, students who are potentially proficient or on the cusp of meeting AYP targets, and students who have achieved proficiency and are ready for enrichment—other schools have, out of expediency or perceived necessity, only focused their support efforts on students with the greatest potential to pass state tests and boost the school's AYP. Using RTI in this way—to boost test scores—is shortsighted, and it risks derailing the transformative, long-term power of RTI-based systems of support in favor of short-term gain. Such prioritizing of resources and supports for the students closest to achieving proficiency on state tests raises ethical and professional questions as well. Is it acceptable to choose to prioritize resources for a subset of students? Is AYP even a worthy target? Does it represent a level of mastery that we desire for our students, and does it represent college or career readiness or another laudable expectation?

Many well-meaning and relatively well-performing schools have applied the principles of RTI to only those grade levels tested by the state under NCLB, usually third grade and above. What these schools fail to consider is that most students attend school for three years prior to taking state tests in third grade, and the most successful systems of support for students are those that recognize that prevention is the best intervention (Buffum et al., 2009, 2012). In addition, the tools associated with RTI—universal screening assessments, progress monitoring tests, evidence-based strategies and programs—are most robust and numerous in the early grades. The tools of RTI are readily available in K–3, more so than in other grades. Yet educators often devote too little attention to RTI in the early elementary years.

By not implementing RTI in the early grades—from kindergarten through grade 3—educators are missing a golden opportunity. This book examines why earlier supports are desirable, illustrates how RTI-based supports can be used in early grades, and explores what such prevention looks like in practice.

What Is RTI?

RTI is a framework for school reform (Khan & Mellard, 2008) that helps educators answer the following four questions:

1. About which students do we have concerns?

2. In what areas do we have concerns?

3. What are we currently doing to support the student and meet the student's needs? What supports will we provide in the future?

4. Has the student responded to the instruction and interventions (the supports) that we have been providing?

The fourth question is critical. The future supports schools provide to students should be based on students' responses to the instruction and interventions they currently receive. If students, at any level of readiness, are responding well to the instruction and supports they are receiving, then schools should continue to provide them. However, when a student's progress and performance are not adequate, then something different must be done; educators must provide more intensive intervention and support—with a sense of urgency—so that students receive the level of support needed to make adequate progress.

There will always be students who don't reach targets on time, so educators must be ready. Schools must establish structures and supports so that there are fewer obstacles for students and teachers when students require more time and resources. Educators can, with a great deal of success, predict and anticipate the following:

- What skills will require attention
- What strategies and resources they can use to meet those skill gaps
- Which staff members can best be freed to provide support
- When supports can be provided
- Approximately how many students will require support
- Which specific students might need support

The importance of early prevention and intervention is outlined in the Individuals with Disabilities Education Improvement Act (IDEIA) of 2004: school districts may use up to 15 percent of their special education dollars, and the human and material resources they fund, to serve students who are not in special education, a process known as early intervening services (EIS). The law specifically encourages schools to focus these special education–funded supports for students not in special education in K–3.

In addition to the emphasis IDEA places on early, K–3 supports, other research and policy recommendations clearly state that students should receive explicit interventions early and that children in kindergarten through third grade are developmentally and cognitively ready for the reading, writing, and mathematics standards and skills that are most essential. This research is discussed in more detail in chapters 1, 2, and 3.

In order to achieve success, educators must continuously strive to embrace two essential practices. First, they must commit to working collaboratively and with a sense of compromise. There are no other practices in education for which there is such unanimity of support, yet a lack of collaboration among teachers continues to sabotage the efforts of schools (Barth, 1991; DuFour, DuFour, & Eaker, 2008; Marzano, 2003). Teacher success often corresponds to the extent to which teachers within a grade level or school work collaboratively, whether they collaborate to improve instructional practice or incorporate RTI practices into their classrooms.

Second, educators must collaboratively determine which standards and skills are most critical for students to master and collaboratively reach consensus on what level of student performance will represent mastery. This is necessary if students are to think critically, problem solve, and explore standards with a rigorous level of depth and complexity. As Richard Elmore notes, "You can only assure that [students master tasks of high cognitive demand] if you have a manageable number of things to teach" (2010, p. 6). The practice of determining essential priorities is in fact critical for all great organizations. As Jim Collins notes in his book *Good to Great*, "The key to success is not innovation; it is 'simplicity and diligence' applied fiercely to our highest priorities" (2001, p. 104).

In addition, Austin Buffum, Mike Mattos, and Chris Weber identify Four Cs—four principles—that are needed for schools to successfully sustain RTI efforts and to ensure high levels of learning for every student (Buffum et al., 2012):

- **Collective responsibility**—A shared belief that the primary responsibility of each member of the organization is to ensure high levels of learning for every child. Thinking is guided by the question, "Why are we here?"

- **Concentrated instruction**—A systematic process of identifying essential knowledge and skills that all students must master to learn at high levels, and determining the specific learning needs for each child to get there. Thinking is guided by the question, "Where do we need to go?"

- **Convergent assessment**—An ongoing process of collectively analyzing targeted evidence to determine the specific learning needs of each child and the effectiveness of the instruction the child receives in meeting these needs. Thinking is guided by the question, "Where are we now?"

- **Certain access**—A systematic process that guarantees every student will receive the time and support needed to learn at high levels. Thinking is guided by the question, "How do we get every child there?"

An RTI system infused with collective responsibility, concentrated instruction, convergent assessment, and certain access has the capability to transform schooling at all grade levels, but such a framework is rarely used in kindergarten through third grade. Lack of maturity, lack of developmental readiness, and lack of English language proficiency are not legitimate excuses to delay intensive supports. Virtually all learning difficulties students encounter during schooling can be efficiently and successfully addressed in the early grades if educators take steps to identify students in need and determine the areas in which they require support. When educators commit to providing this support with intensity, a sense of urgency, and the expectation that schools and students will be successful in achieving the highest levels of mastery and depth of understanding, students will succeed.

A fundamental premise of this book is that prevention is the best intervention. However, no single preventative measure has the potential to be as effective as superb instruction in the early grades coupled with high expectations for every student.

Why Read This Book?

This book is for educators—teachers, specialists, administrators, and support personnel—who are interested in authentically translating research into practice. Educators have known what to do for years, but implementing and sustaining best practice has proven to be trickier. It's not enough to know about best practice; if it's not visible in every classroom, in every school, and through student performance, then it has no impact.

This book presents best practices and strategies in reading, writing, and mathematics instruction for kindergarten through grade 3, as well as best practices for English learners and for supporting students' social, behavioral, language, and fine-motor skills. The scope is broad and practical because busy primary teachers and elementary administrators and specialists are rarely at liberty to focus solely on a single content area. Moreover, theory and best intentions are little more than words if they do not lead to results in the classroom. This is a book about doing—for practitioners by a practitioner. Individual teachers, specialists, clinicians, and administrators can use the ideas and resources in this book to improve their craft. Teams of teachers can use this book to collaboratively refine their practice. Principals can use this book to define and organize their work in leading and supporting their staff. District office staff can use this book to begin a dialogue on evidence-based supports for early education.

Chapters 1, 2, and 3 examine the key content and fundamental skills students should obtain in kindergarten through third grade in the areas of reading, writing, and mathematics. These chapters include key research findings and research and policy recommendations as well as reference to and interpretation of the Common Core State Standards (CCSS) and sample tools for ensuring success. These chapters examine how purposefully interconnected teaching and assessing are organized, structured, and supported in effective classrooms and schools. The chapters end with reproducible Guiding Goals checklists to help determine the next steps you will take in your classroom, school, or district RTI-based K–3 program.

Chapter 4 focuses on the critical topic of English learners. It draws on research that has shed new light on key skills and best practices that can significantly improve the supports educators provide to English learners in the early grades.

Chapter 5 describes the role that clinicians play in instruction and intervention in kindergarten through third grade. While psychologists, speech and language pathologists, and occupational therapists may not be in a position to provide direct services to students in these early grades, they can add value to educators' efforts through professional development and structured consultations with classroom teachers.

The best schools embrace collaborative practices, identify and clearly define essential standards and skills, and recognize that striving for continuous improvement is the necessary reality for ensuring students' continued success. They also provide students with high-quality attention and supports in the earliest grades—not just when students are tested for AYP. This book presents a practical argument for this early support, and it offers tools, recommendations, and examples of effective models for educators to implement RTI in kindergarten through grade 3.

CHAPTER 1

Reading

A capacity, and taste, for reading, gives access to whatever has already been discovered by others. It is the key, or one of the keys, to the already solved problems. And not only so. It gives a relish, and facility, for successfully pursuing the [yet] unsolved ones.

ABRAHAM LINCOLN

Reading is the most fundamental and important skill students will master in school. Reading proficiency unlocks information; it allows students to solve problems. Reading feeds reading ability by building vocabulary and background knowledge and sharpening comprehension skills. The sooner a student starts to read, the sooner he or she unlocks the powers and potentials of reading. Educators must recognize that students can be successful phonologically and phonetically at an early age and resist the temptation to exchange rigor for developmentally appropriate discovery—they must embrace both.

Research on Early Reading

Research demonstrates that early, focused academic literacy instruction is linked with higher levels of achievement later in school, as well as higher levels of emotional and social well-being, fewer retentions, reduced juvenile delinquency, and greater adult productivity (Barnett, 2002; Bowman, Donovan, & Burns, 2000; Heckman, 2006; Connor & Tiedemann, 2005; Karoly, Kilburn, & Cannon, 2005; National Institute for Literacy, 2008; Shonkoff & Phillips, 2000; Storch & Whitehurst, 2002; Strickland & Barnett, 2003).

In their *Report of the National Reading Panel*, the National Institute of Child Health and Human Development (2000) determined that many deficiencies in learning to read are the result of inadequate phonemic awareness instruction and that systematic and explicit instruction in phonemic awareness is directly related to improvements in children's reading and spelling. The panel recommends that instruction in phonemic awareness should begin no later than kindergarten and should continue for students who have difficulties identifying phonemes in spoken words. The panel notes that kindergarten students respond well to instruction in phonemic awareness when it is presented in an age-appropriate manner.

The panel also found that explicit phonics instruction from kindergarten through sixth grade leads to improved reading. Systematic phonics instruction in a planned sequence is more effective than teaching phonics when examples appear in text. While the panel concluded that synthetic phonics instruction is most beneficial and is appropriate for all classrooms, it also recommends that the instruction be differentiated among the following types:

- **Analogy phonics**—Teaching unfamiliar words with comparisons to known words (such as reading *brick* by recognizing that *-ick* is contained in the known word *kick*)

- **Analytic phonics**—Teaching to analyze letter-sound relations in previously learned words so that sounds are not pronounced in isolation

- **Embedded phonics**—Teaching phonics skills by embedding phonics instruction in text reading

- **Phonics through spelling**—Teaching to segment words into phonemes and to select letters for those phonemes

- **Synthetic phonics**—Explicitly teaching to convert letters into sounds and blend the sounds to form words

The need for direct and systematic instruction in phonemic awareness and phonics is particularly relevant for students who enter school already behind in reading; instruction and intervention should begin in kindergarten and should continue through the late elementary school years. While all students will benefit from more advanced phonics instruction in the later elementary grades, and late-elementary students for whom reading is challenging will most definitely respond to high-quality intervention, earlier supports are best.

The panel also concluded that guided oral reading is important for the development of reading fluency. Guided oral reading benefits students of all levels as they learn to recognize new words, read accurately and easily, and comprehend what they read. However, the panel did not determine that reading silently to oneself helps improve fluency, although the best readers read silently to themselves more frequently than do poor readers. The panel recommends that vocabulary be taught both separately from text and as encountered in text, and it emphasizes the use of multiple exposure and computer technology. Regarding comprehension, the panel recommends teaching students techniques and strategies to assist with the following:

- **Monitoring**—Learning to be aware of one's understanding
- **Cooperative learning**—Learning reading strategies through collaboration and conversations with other students
- **Use of graphic organizers**—Learning to visually represent thinking
- **Question answering**—Answering questions from the teacher and receiving immediate feedback
- **Question generation**—Asking questions of oneself about a story
- **Story structure**—Using a story's structure to recall content and answer questions
- **Summarization**—Learning to integrate ideas and generalize from text

Finally, the panel suggests that while computer technology can supplement text-to-speech interactions, teachers are the key diagnosticians and decision makers when furthering the reading skills of students.

Key Reading Content

The final goal of reading instruction is comprehension—we teach phonological awareness, phonics, fluency, vocabulary, and comprehension skills and strategies so that students learn to make meaning through metacognitive interactions with text. Educators must not lose sight of this final goal; however, they must also focus attention on shorter-term goals in the early grades. The Common Core State Standards (CCSS; National Governors Association Center for Best Practices & Council of Chief State School Officers, 2010a, 2010b) provide a consistent, clear understanding of what students are expected to learn at each grade level. Standards for reading in kindergarten through grade 3 are summarized in table 1.1 (page 10).

Kindergarten Common Core Reading Standards

In kindergarten, concepts of print remain a significant grade-level goal. Students should produce and identify rhymes; count, blend, and segment syllables; segment and blend onsets and rimes; segment phonemes within consonant-vowel-consonant (CVC) words; and add and substitute phonemes to and from words.

Naming and recognizing uppercase and lowercase letters, connecting consonant letter names to sounds, connecting vowel names to long and short sounds, and reading high-frequency words are kindergarten reading goals.

In the area of comprehension and vocabulary, goals are questioning; summarizing the main idea and details; describing characters, settings, and events; determining types of text; identifying and defining the roles of authors and illustrators; and comparing and contrasting to understand story structure and comprehend text.

Table 1.1: Synthesis of Common Core State Standards for Reading Literature, Information, and Foundations

Kindergarten	First Grade	Second Grade	Third Grade
With prompting and support, ask and answer questions about key details.	Ask and answer questions about key details.	Ask and answer such questions as who, what, where, when, why, and how to demonstrate understanding of key details.	Ask and answer questions to demonstrate understanding, referring explicitly to the text as the basis for the answers.
With prompting and support, retell familiar stories, including key details.	Retell stories, including key details, and demonstrate understanding of their central message or lesson.	Recount stories, including fables and folktales from diverse cultures, and determine their central message, lesson, or moral.	Recount stories, including fables, folktales, and myths from diverse cultures. Determine the central message, lesson, or moral, and explain how it is conveyed through key details.
With prompting, identify the main topic and retell key details and the reasons an author gives to support points.	Identify the main topic and retell key details and the reasons an author gives to support points.	Identify the main topic (or purpose) of a multiparagraph text and the focus of paragraphs, including what the author wants to answer, explain, or describe, and the reasons an author gives to support points.	Determine the main idea; recount key details and explain how they support the main idea.
With prompting, identify characters, settings, and major events.	Describe characters, settings, and major events, using key details.	Describe how characters in a story respond to major events and challenges.	Describe characters in a story (traits, motivations, feelings) and explain how actions contribute to the sequence of events.
Ask and answer questions about decoding unknown words.	Identify words and phrases in stories or poems that suggest feelings or appeal to the senses.	Describe how words and phrases (beats, alliteration, rhymes, repeated lines) supply rhythm and meaning in a story, poem, or song.	Determine the meaning of words and phrases, distinguishing literal from nonliteral language.

With prompting, ask and answer questions about the meaning of unknown words.	Ask and answer questions to help determine or clarify the meaning of words and phrases.	Determine the meaning of words and phrases.	Determine the meaning of academic and domain-specific words and phrases.
Recognize common types of texts (storybooks, poems).	Explain differences between books that tell stories and books that give information.	Describe the structure of a story, including how the beginning introduces the story and the ending concludes the action.	Refer to parts of stories, dramas, and poems when writing or speaking about text; describe how each successively builds; and describe the connection between sentences and paragraphs (comparison, cause and effect, sequence).
With prompting, name the author and illustrator and define the role of each.	Identify who is telling the story at various points in a text.	Acknowledge differences in points of view of characters, including speaking in a different voice for each character when reading dialogue aloud.	Distinguish the narrator's point of view from those of the characters and the students' own point of view from that of the author.
With prompting, describe the relationship between illustrations and the story.	Use illustrations and details in a story to describe its characters, setting, or events, and distinguish between information provided by illustrations and by words.	Use information gained from illustrations and words to understand characters, setting, or plot, and explain how each contribute to and clarify a text.	Explain how illustrations (maps, photographs) contribute to what is conveyed by the words (create mood, emphasize aspects of a character or setting) to demonstrate understanding (where, when, why, and how key events occur).

Source: NGA & CCSSO, 2010a.

continued →

Kindergarten	First Grade	Second Grade	Third Grade
With prompting, compare and contrast the adventures and experiences of characters in familiar stories and between two texts on the same topic (in illustrations, descriptions, or procedures).	Compare and contrast the adventures and experiences of characters in stories and between two texts on the same topic (in illustrations, descriptions, or procedures).	Compare and contrast two or more versions of the same story (such as Cinderella stories) by different authors or from different cultures and the most important points presented by two texts on the same topic.	Compare and contrast themes, settings, and plots of stories written by the same author about similar characters (books from a series) and the most important points and key details presented in two texts on the same topic.
With prompting, describe the connection between two individuals, events, ideas, or pieces of information.	Describe the connection between two individuals, events, ideas, or pieces of information.	Describe the connection between historical events, scientific ideas, or steps in technical procedures.	Describe the relationship between historical events, scientific ideas, or steps in technical procedures, using language that pertains to time, sequence, and cause/effect.
Actively engage in group reading activities.	With prompting, read prose, poetry, and informational texts.	Read and comprehend stories, poetry, and informational texts, including history and social studies, science, and technical texts.	Read and comprehend stories, dramas, poetry, and informational texts, including history and social studies, science, and technical texts.
Identify the front cover, back cover, and title page.	Use various text features (headings, tables of contents, glossaries, electronic menus, icons) to locate key facts or information.	Use various text features (captions, bold print, subheadings, glossaries, indexes, electronic menus, icons) to locate key facts or information efficiently.	Use text features and search tools (key words, sidebars, hyperlinks) to locate information relevant to a given topic efficiently.

continued →

Understand the organization and features of print. Recognize distinguishing features of a sentence (first word, capitalization, ending punctuation).	Understand spoken words, syllables, and phonemes. Distinguish long from short vowels in spoken single-syllable words. Orally produce single-syllable words by blending phonemes, including consonant blends. Isolate and pronounce initial, medial-vowel, and final phonemes in spoken single-syllable words. Segment spoken single-syllable words into their complete sequence of individual phonemes.
Understand the organization and features of print. Follow words left to right, top to bottom, and page by page. Recognize that spoken words are represented in writing by specific sequences of letters. Understand that words are separated by spaces. Name all upper- and lowercase letters of the alphabet.	Understand spoken words, syllables, and phonemes. Recognize and produce rhyming words. Count, pronounce, blend, and segment syllables in spoken words. Blend and segment onsets and rimes of single-syllable spoken words. Isolate and pronounce the initial, medial-vowel, and final phonemes in three-phoneme words (not including CVCs ending with /l/, /r/, or /x/). Add or substitute individual phonemes in one-syllable words to make new words.

Kindergarten	First Grade	Second Grade	Third Grade
Apply phonics and word analysis skills in decoding words. Demonstrate knowledge of one-to-one letter-sound correspondences by producing the most frequent sound for each consonant. Associate the long and short sounds with common spellings for the five major vowels. Read common high-frequency words by sight (the, of, to, you, she, my, is, are, do, does). Distinguish between similarly spelled words by identifying the sounds of letters that differ.	Apply phonics and word analysis skills in decoding words. Know spelling-sound correspondences for common consonant digraphs. Decode regularly spelled one-syllable words. Know final –e and common vowel team conventions for long vowel sounds. Know every syllable must have a vowel sound to determine number of syllables. Decode two-syllable words by breaking words into syllables. Read words with inflectional endings. Read irregularly spelled words.	Apply phonics and word analysis skills in decoding words. Distinguish long and short vowels when reading regularly spelled one-syllable words. Know spelling-sound correspondences for common vowel teams. Decode regularly spelled two-syllable words with long vowels. Decode words with common prefixes and suffixes. Identify words with inconsistent but common spelling-sound correspondences. Read irregularly spelled words.	Apply phonics and word analysis skills in decoding words. Know the meaning of the most common prefixes and derivational suffixes. Decode words with common Latin suffixes. Decode multisyllable words. Read irregularly spelled words.
Read emergent-reader texts with purpose and understanding.	Read with the accuracy and fluency to support comprehension. Read on-level text with purpose and understanding. Read text orally with accuracy, at an appropriate rate, and with expression on successive readings. Use context to confirm or self-correct word recognition and understanding, rereading as necessary.	Read with the accuracy and fluency to support comprehension. Read on-level text with purpose and understanding. Read on-level text orally with accuracy, at an appropriate rate, and with expression on successive readings. Use context to confirm or self-correct word recognition and understanding, rereading as necessary.	Read with the accuracy and fluency to support comprehension. Read on-level text with purpose and understanding. Read on-level prose and poetry orally with accuracy, at an appropriate rate, and with expression. Use context to confirm or self-correct word recognition and understanding, rereading as necessary.

The CCSS for reading in kindergarten match the recommendations of the National Reading Panel—there is an early focus on phonological awareness and phonics. This can be accomplished in creative and developmentally appropriate ways, as explored in the instruction section later in this chapter. In addition, comprehension instruction must be robust and present for all students in kindergarten, particularly for students already deemed to be at risk in reading, as determined through deficits in phonological awareness. Denying kindergarten students access to core comprehension instruction because they are receiving pullout intervention for phonological awareness needs violates the principles of RTI and will harm students' reading development.

First-Grade Common Core Reading Standards

In first grade, goals for phonological awareness include orally blending and segmenting one-syllable words. First-grade students should be able to identify and fluently read consonant digraphs; final –e long vowels and vowel digraphs; inflective endings; and one- and two-syllable words, including irregularly spelled words. Students should also be able to determine syllables within words and read fluently, with accuracy, expression, and self-corrections and at an appropriate rate.

In the areas of comprehension and vocabulary, first-grade goals for fiction and nonfiction texts are questioning; summarizing the main idea and details; describing characters, settings, and events with illustrations and key written details; identifying sensory language; determining point of view; using contexts to determine the meaning of words and phrases; and comparing and contrasting characters, illustrations, events, and ideas.

First-grade students should fluently read and comprehend both narrative and informational texts containing both one- and two-syllable words and complex structures and uses of language.

Second-Grade Common Core Reading Standards

Second-grade students should be able to distinguish between long and short vowels in one- and two-syllable words; read vowel digraphs and diphthongs; identify and read prefixes and suffixes; and read fluently, with accuracy, expression, and self-corrections and at an appropriate rate.

Second-grade comprehension and vocabulary goals include questioning; summarizing the main idea and details of paragraphs and multiparagraph texts; recalling fables and identifying the moral; describing character changes and the differing points of views of characters; identifying rhythm and meter; sequencing narratives; using text features, diagrams, and illustrations to comprehend; describing sequential connections between events, ideas, and steps; using contexts to determine the meaning of words and phrases; and comparing and contrasting multiple versions of the same story from different authors and two texts on the same topic.

Third-Grade Common Core Reading Standards

Third-grade students should be able to identify and read common derivational Latin affixes, read multisyllabic words, and read fluently, with accuracy, expression, and self-corrections and at an appropriate rate. Third-grade students' comprehension and vocabulary goals include the following:

- Referencing text when asking and answering questions
- Summarizing the main idea and details of text
- Recalling fables and identifying the moral with supporting details
- Describing characters' impacts on causes and effects in a story and the differing points of views of characters
- Identifying chapters, stanzas, and scenes
- Using text features and search tools to locate information
- Distinguishing the reader's point of view from that of the author, narrator, and characters
- Identifying text structures such as comparisons, sequences, and cause and effect that help communicate the main idea
- Using illustrations to answer key questions about events
- Using contexts to determine the meaning of general academic and domain-specific words and phrases
- Distinguishing literal from nonliteral language
- Comparing and contrasting themes, settings, and plots of stories written by the same author about the same characters, as well as important points and key details presented in two texts on the same topic

Second- and third-grade key content continues to focus on phonics and advanced decoding skills. Moreover, students are expected to demonstrate proficiency with complex and sophisticated text and text structures.

The Scope and Sequence of Reading

Throughout the early grades, a few key skills receive consistent focus. Phonics and decoding begin in kindergarten and continue through third grade. Oral reading fluency is specifically identified as a key indicator of overall reading achievement (Fuchs, Fuchs, Hosp, & Jenkins, 2001), although many comprehensive literacy programs lack resources for explicitly teaching fluency. Main idea and details, summarizing (which is a strategy that complements the identification of the main idea), and comparing and contrasting are constant features of comprehension content from kindergarten to third grade.

Another helpful way of envisioning the scope and sequence of reading content is John Shefelbine and Gerry Shiel's Framework for Reading (1990), as shown in table 1.2.

Table 1.2: Shefelbine and Shiel's Framework for Reading

Decoding				
Word-Recognition Strategies			Fluency	
Concepts about print	Phonemic awareness	Phonics	Sight words	Automaticity
Comprehension				
Academic Language			Comprehension Strategies	
Background knowledge	Vocabulary	Syntax/text structure	Comprehension monitoring	(Re)organizing text

Source: Shefelbine & Shiel, 1990. Reprinted with permission.

While the five major domains of reading (phonemic awareness, phonics, fluency, vocabulary, and comprehension) are present, the secondary descriptors (word-recognition strategies, fluency, academic language, and comprehension strategies) are an alternative way in which decoding and comprehension can be categorized. The tertiary descriptors introduce important concepts (for example, background knowledge and syntax and text structure) that are useful in supporting readers.

Teachers must examine the standards (whether the CCSS or individual state or district standards), identify the key content, and unpack the standards. Then teacher teams must establish a scope and sequence for instruction, perhaps in the form of a curriculum map. Schools that use comprehensive reading programs from large publishers may be inclined to adopt much of the scope and sequence recommendations included in these programs, but teachers should carefully examine the appropriateness of lessons and activities and the scope and sequence in relation to their work in identifying and sequencing key content.

A sample scope and sequence of key reading content for September through January for each grade level appears in figure 1.1 (page 18). It is based on National Institute of Child Health and Human Development (2000) recommendations, and the instruction is ordered so as to best serve all students with high levels and depth of learning. (Visit **go.solution-tree.com/rti** to see a complete sample scope and sequence document.)

	September	October	November	December	January
Kindergarten	• Understand spoken words, syllables, and phonemes. • Recognize and produce rhyming words. • Decode unknown words. • Determine the meaning of unknown words and key details in stories. • Understand features of print. • Know that words are represented by sequences of letters. • Actively engage in group reading activities.	• Manipulate syllables, onsets, and rimes in spoken words. • Name all upper- and lowercase letters. • Retell familiar stories, providing key details. • Decode unknown words. • Determine the meaning of unknown words and key details in stories. • Actively engage in group reading activities.	• Isolate and pronounce the initial, medial-vowel, and final phonemes in three-phoneme words. • Identify the main topic and retell key details. • Decode unknown words. • Determine the meaning of unknown words and key details in stories. • Actively engage in group reading activities.	• Add or substitute individual phonemes in one-syllable words to make new words. • Decode unknown words. • Determine the meaning of unknown words and key details in stories • Recognize common types of texts. • Actively engage in group reading activities.	• Apply phonics skills in decoding. • Know one-to-one letter-sound correspondences for consonants. • Decode unknown words. • Determine the meaning of unknown words and key details in stories. • Name and define the role of the author and illustrator. • Actively engage in group reading activities.
First Grade	• Understand spoken words, syllables, and phonemes.	• Apply phonics in decoding.	• Apply phonics in decoding.	• Apply phonics in decoding.	• Apply phonics in decoding.

		Second Grade	
• Apply phonics skills in decoding. • Read with accuracy and fluency to support comprehension. • Use text features to locate key facts or information. • Understand features of print. • Recognize features of a sentence. • Identify portions of text that relate to feelings or the senses. • Clarify the meaning of words and phrases. • Read prose, poetry, and informational texts.	• Manipulate phonemes in spoken single-syllable words. • Read text orally with accuracy, at an appropriate rate, and with expression. • Identify the main topic and retell key details and reasons. • Identify portions of text that relate to feelings or the senses. • Clarify the meaning of words and phrases. • Read prose, poetry, and informational texts.	• Segment words into phonemes. • Use context and rereading to clarify word understanding. • Identify portions of text that relate to feelings or the senses. • Clarify the meaning of words and phrases. • Explain differences between books that tell stories and books that give information. • Read prose, poetry, and informational texts.	• Know spelling-sound correspondences for consonant digraphs. • Identify portions of text that relate to feelings or the senses. • Clarify the meaning of words and phrases. • Identify who is telling the story at various points in a text. • Read prose, poetry, and informational texts.
• Apply phonics in decoding.	• Apply phonics in decoding.	• Apply phonics in decoding.	• Apply phonics in decoding.

Figure 1.1: Sample scope and sequence chart for grades K–3.

Source: NGA & CCSSO, 2010a.

continued ↓

Second Grade

September	October	November	December	January
• Distinguish long and short vowels in one-syllable words.	• Know spelling-sound correspondences for vowel teams.	• Decode regularly spelled two-syllable words with long vowels.	• Decode words with common prefixes and suffixes.	• Read words with inconsistent but common spelling-sound correspondences.
• Read with accuracy and fluency to support comprehension.	• Read text with purpose and understanding.	• Read text orally with accuracy, at an appropriate rate, and with expression.	• Use context and rereading to clarify word understanding.	• Identify the main topic of a multi-paragraph text and the focus of paragraphs.
• Ask and answer who, what, where, when, and why questions in understanding of key details.	• Recount stories and determine their central message or moral.	• Identify the main topic of a multi-paragraph text and the focus of paragraphs.	• Identify the main topic of a multi-paragraph text and the focus of paragraphs.	• Describe how words and phrases supply rhythm and meaning.
• Use text features to locate key facts or information.	• Describe how words and phrases supply rhythm and meaning.	• Describe how words and phrases supply rhythm and meaning.	• Describe how words and phrases supply rhythm and meaning.	• Clarify the meaning of words and phrases.
• Describe how words and phrases supply rhythm and meaning.	• Clarify the meaning of words and phrases.	• Clarify the meaning of words and phrases.	• Clarify the meaning of words and phrases.	• Analyze differences in points of view for characters.
• Determine the meaning of words and phrases.	• Read and comprehend stories, poetry, and informational texts.	• Read and comprehend stories, poetry, and informational texts.	• Describe the structure of a story, including the beginning and ending.	• Read and comprehend stories, poetry, and informational texts.
• Read and comprehend stories, poetry, and informational texts.			• Read and comprehend stories, poetry, and informational texts.	

Third Grade

• Apply phonics in decoding.	• Apply phonics in decoding.	• Apply phonics and word analysis skills in decoding words.	• Apply phonics and word analysis skills in decoding words.	• Apply phonics and word analysis skills in decoding words.
• Read with the accuracy and fluency to support comprehension.	• Know the meaning of common prefixes and derivational suffixes.	• Decode words with common Latin suffixes.	• Read irregularly spelled words.	• Clarify the meaning of words and phrases, distinguishing literal from nonliteral language.
• Ask and answer questions to demonstrate understanding, referring to the text for answers.	• Read text with purpose and understanding.	• Decode multisyllable words.	• Use context and rereading to clarify word understanding.	• Determine the meaning of academic and domain-specific words and phrases.
• Use text features and search tools to locate information.	• Recount stories from diverse cultures; determine the lesson or moral through key details.	• Read text orally with accuracy, at an appropriate rate, and with expression.	• Clarify the meaning of words and phrases, distinguishing literal from nonliteral language.	• Distinguish the point of view of the narrator, characters, reader, and author.
• Clarify the meaning of words and phrases, distinguishing literal from nonliteral language.	• Clarify the meaning of words and phrases, distinguishing literal from nonliteral language.	• Determine the main idea; recount key details and their support of the main idea.	• Determine the meaning of academic and domain-specific words and phrases.	• Read and comprehend stories, poetry, and informational texts.
• Determine the meaning of academic and domain-specific words and phrases.	• Determine the meaning of academic and domain-specific words and phrases.	• Clarify the meaning of words and phrases, distinguishing literal from nonliteral language.	• Refer to stories when writing or speaking about text; describe how stories build; describe connection (comparison, cause/effect, sequence).	
• Read and comprehend stories, poetry, and informational texts.	• Read and comprehend stories, poetry, and informational texts.	• Determine the meaning of academic and domain-specific words and phrases.	• Read and comprehend stories, poetry, and informational texts.	
		• Read and comprehend stories, poetry, and informational texts.		

Reading Instruction

The key content educators expect students to master is of critical importance. Perhaps even more important, however, are the ways in which, and the depth to which, educators help students achieve mastery of the key content. In the 21st century, American education has undergone curricularization. While the quality and research base of programs and curricula have improved, an unfortunate consequence of the change has been that instruction and lesson design have devolved to take on a subservient role in relation to curriculum. Prescribed lesson scripts too often obliterate the craft of teaching. Furthermore, differentiation is often forgotten and can be more difficult with a one-size-fits-all approach.

There are two keys to instruction described in this section of the chapter that fit within the RTI framework: the overall structure of lesson design, and the instructional strategies used to help all students access content. Textbooks do not teach students; teachers do. Lessons must be designed and cognitively planned so that teachers first model problem solving and critical thinking. Then, greater responsibility for learning can be gradually released to students, first with guidance, frequent checks for understanding, and immediate, specific corrective feedback. A gradual release of responsibility lesson design is described in the following section.

Figure 1.2: Deductive lesson design.

Source: Fisher & Frey, 2008. Adapted with permission. Learn more about ASCD at www.ascd.org.

The Gradual Release of Responsibility Model

The most cogent type of lesson design is the gradual release of responsibility model (Fisher & Frey, 2007). Douglas Fisher and Nancy Frey's model is evidence-based for use in K–12 classrooms and uses common sense language. This model and its vocabulary are used throughout this book. With the gradual release of responsibility model, teachers open a lesson by modeling the behaviors of expert learners. Through enthusiastic and animated metacognitive modeling or think-alouds, teachers demonstrate for students the ways in which learning occurs. Figure 1.2 shows the steps of this deductive lesson design.

Both the deductive lesson design described in this section and the inductive lesson design described later share important attributes. Both lessons include opportunities for students to observe a model learner—the teacher—as the teacher thinks aloud and metacognitively models critical thinking and problem solving. In addition, teachers and students solve problems together. In a deductive lesson, lessons open with greater levels of teacher guidance but include less teacher voice as checks for understanding reveal increasing levels of student knowledge; in an inductive lesson, lessons open with student inquiry before teacher voice begins. Both lessons are planned and structured, and in both, students have frequent opportunities to talk with one another; at least 50 percent of the lesson includes student voice. Finally, the pace and progress of both lessons are based on data: checks for understanding that indicate whether or not students are responding to the teacher's instruction. If students are not responding to instruction, if they are not learning, the teacher takes responsibility for adjusting the instruction before asking students to work at greater levels of independence.

A deductive gradual release of responsibility lesson design supports students within an RTI-framework in two primary ways. First, core, Tier 1 instruction is systematic, organized, and proceeds based on evidence. After students observe teachers problem solve in the I Do It phase, the We Do It Together phase proceeds in a step-by-step manner based on the teacher's assessment of students' developing understanding. Feedback can be immediate and specific. Teachers do not allow students to proceed to the You Do It Together and You Do It Alone phases unless they have demonstrated a sufficient level of mastery. The second primary way in which such a model supports students in an RTI-framework is the opportunity for immediate, targeted intervention for specific students within the lesson itself. If students are assessed by the teacher to insufficiently understand content toward the conclusion of the We Do It Together and You Do It Together phase, then they do not necessarily proceed with their classmates to the You Do It Alone phase; instead, they work with the teacher in a small group during this phase, receiving more guidance and support. Students may be informally assessed by the teacher earlier in the lesson, toward the conclusion of the We Do It Together phase, and receive more guidance and support during the You Do It Together phase before receiving differentiated tasks to complete during the You Do It Alone phase.

A key part of lesson design is the actual task students complete as they try to understand the material presented to them from the curriculum. Walter Doyle (1983) proposes:

> This is cognitive work but it might occur within individual heads only or include the understandings that grow out of interactions among students or between students and teachers. This work could range from memorization and making obvious connections between what one already knows to evaluation, application, problem solving and critical thinking. (p. 167)

The task matters and should be differentiated based on student readiness and need. The task with which a student engages is the center of the classroom, as shown in figure 1.3 (page 24). Meaningful, high-level relationships between the key content, the teacher, and the student all inform and are informed by the nature of the task (Elmore, 2008).

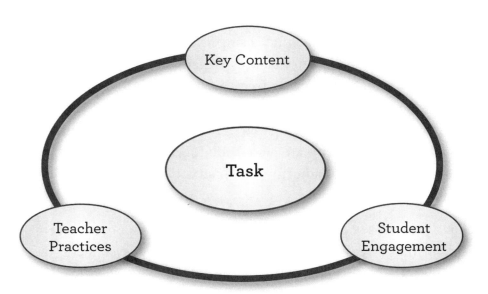

Figure 1.3: Elmore's instructional core.

Source: Elmore, 2008. Reprinted with permission.

Key content in reading as identified by the CCSS or state or district standards must be complemented by effective teacher practices, such as the gradual release of responsibility model, and structured within a well-designed lesson. While there are numerous effective practices, the following simple routines are high-leverage strategies that can be used across content and contribute to high levels of student engagement (Fisher & Frey, 2007; Leithwood, McAdie, Bascia, & Rodrigue, 2005; Marzano, Pickering, & Pollock, 2001; Newmann & Wehlage, 1993):

- Explicitly teaching students to compare and contrast and summarize
- Using graphic organizers
- Providing feedback (after checking for understanding)

In the I Do It phase, the quantity and quality of teacher talk is critical; teacher talk should be limited and should focus on demonstration and modeling, followed by the introduction of significant student voice (students verbally engaged during 50 percent of the lesson) and teacher feedback (Duke & Pearson, 2002; Pearson & Gallagher, 1983). After the teacher inputs and models (the I Do It phase), students should be guided to think about the content, to pair their thoughts with a partner, and to share their answers with the teacher and other students during the We Do It Together phase; this sharing provides an invaluable check for understanding to guide the pace of instruction. The tasks that frame the key content are introduced during the I Do It phase. Tasks should not change dramatically throughout the lesson.

Many teachers express frustration when tasks that students are asked to complete with their peers (during the You Do It Together phase) or independently (during the You Do It Alone phase) lead to dozens of tiny hands raised accompanied by quizzical looks, despite the wonderful way in which the content was taught. What has happened? Often, teacher practices during the I Do It phase do not match basal textbook worksheets. This disconnect leads to confusion (students raising their hands, completing the task incorrectly, or disengaging from the assignment) and places student learning at risk. Thus, while students should ultimately be able to transfer their learning to unique contexts, the continuity of a task from the beginning to the end of the lesson is a critical consideration.

Deductive Lesson Design

A deductive lesson design, based on the gradual release of responsibility model, is highly structured. Teachers must ensure that deductive, gradual release models are firmly in place because student voice, student activity, and student engagement must be more present in classrooms than is currently the norm. Research of typical classrooms reveals that students are active or talking much less than half the instructional time (Cazden, 2001). The goal must be that students are talking (to each other, to the teacher, or to themselves, through oral rehearsal) during at least 50 percent of the lesson (Fisher & Frey, 2007).

In addition, students have been shown to learn more when routines and structures are in place (Black & Wiliam, 1998; Duke & Pearson, 2002; Hattie, 2009). Routines and structures help create a safe environment and allow for students to assume responsibility for their learning. Unfortunately, many lessons follow the "I Do It, Now You Do It" model, in which the release of responsibility is anything but gradual, teacher-to-student and student-to-student interaction is minimal, and teachers do not have the opportunity to check for student understanding (Fisher & Frey, 2007). Many lessons too often follow the "We Do It Together Only" model in which the whole class completes an assignment with little teacher modeling and few opportunities for students to practice at increasing levels of independence. Deductive lesson designs that follow a gradual release of responsibility format also provide opportunities for teachers to provide immediate and specific corrective feedback to students, as well as opportunities for teachers to formally and informally check for understanding.

What follows is a sample deductive lesson from second grade for which the Common Core standard (RL.2.3) is, "Describe how characters in a story respond to major events and challenges" from the Reading Standards for Literature in grade 2, and the objective is, "Students will be able to identify and interpret cause and effect to assist in making meaning of text" (NGA & CCSSO, 2010a).

Why Do It?

The teacher introduces the topic of the story that the class will be reading—*Make Way for Ducklings* by Robert McCloskey (1941)—activating background knowledge, connecting the theme to other stories that the class has read (such as *Matilda* by Roald Dahl [1998], *Fox and His Friends* by Edward Marshall [1994], and *Frog and Toad Together* by Arnold Lobel [1972]), and providing visual supports to key vocabulary from the story with which the students may not be familiar.

The teacher also introduces students to the concept of cause and effect, providing a graphic organizer to represent this comprehension skill (Marzano, Pickering, & Pollock, 2001; Moss, 2004). The teacher introduces the concept of cause and effect with a scenario with which students may already be familiar: failing to complete homework. Figure 1.4 shows how the teacher activates prior knowledge during the Why Do It? phase.

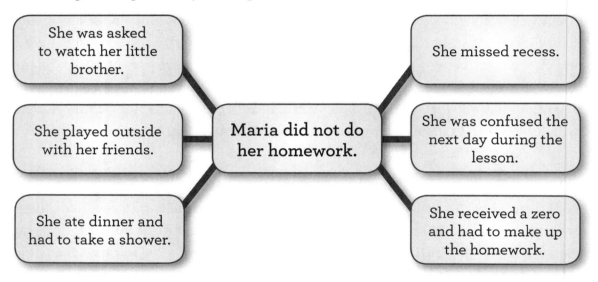

Figure 1.4: Activating prior knowledge during the Why Do It? phase.

During this introduction of cause and effect, the teacher is animated and metacognitive, modeling how she determines possible causes and effects of Maria not doing her homework.

I Do It

Next, the teacher models the concept of cause and effect using a section of text from *Make Way for Ducklings* (1941). After reading several selections that provide suitable examples of cause and effect, the teacher identifies the key events of the sections of the text, and then models the identification of the causes and effects, while also interpreting the meanings of the passages. (While the examples in this chapter include three causes and three effects, teachers can use fewer or more.) Figure 1.5 shows a blank cause-and-effect graphic organizer. The objective of the lesson is to equip students with a skill (determining cause and effect) that will assist them in making meaning of what they read—that is, in comprehending the text.

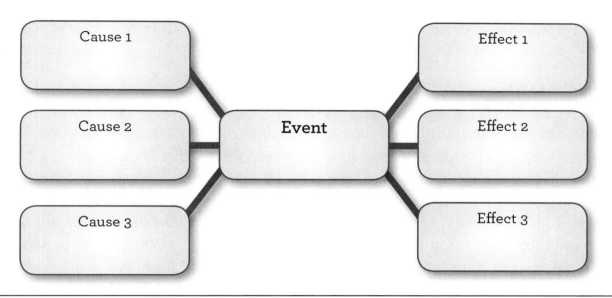

Figure 1.5: Cause-and-effect graphic organizer.

We Do It Together

Next, the teacher and the class read another section of the story together, combining teacher read-aloud, student reading, buddy reading, and choral reading. Using think-pair-share strategies (Lyman, 1981), the teacher asks students to first think about the main event of the section, then pair their response with their partner (with the student designated as partner A sharing first, followed by the student designated as partner B), before randomly selecting a pair to share with the class. The teacher records the responses of several pairs before recording one response on a new graphic organizer identical to the organizer shown in figure 1.5. This same process is used to identify key causes and key effects and concludes with students interpreting the meaning of the passage through the structural feature of cause and effect. Through this process, students have numerous opportunities to think and express themselves both orally and in writing. The teacher has numerous opportunities to hear student responses, providing immediate and specific corrective feedback in a timely manner and checking for understanding to determine the appropriate pace of the lesson.

You Do It Together

The teacher then asks students to read a preselected portion of the story in pairs. The pairs take turns reading the passage and creating their own graphic organizer, starting with the event and moving on to causes and effects, with first partner A and then partner B contributing. The teacher walks the room, providing guidance when necessary, contributing ideas about the event (or causes or effects) when necessary, correcting misunderstandings, identifying students who may need supplemental support, and documenting the performance of students (marking individual students' graphic organizers with a red, green, or blue dot based on their mastery). As students finish, the teacher randomly calls on several pairs to complete a classwide graphic organizer for the passage.

You Do It Alone

Based on her evaluation of student performance during the You Do It Together phase and her understanding of student needs, the teacher assigns each student to a different group (identified by color) for independent practice. Students are given a fluency folder that contains tasks that are differentiated based on their readiness levels and needs, including fluency passages and differentiated word study spelling tasks. The teacher places different activities within students' folders regularly. In addition to the differentiated tasks within their fluency folders, students also complete a new cause-and-effect graphic organizer. The red group will read a slightly more complex passage and then complete a blank graphic organizer. The green group will read an on-level passage and then complete a graphic organizer for which the key event has been provided. The blue group will read a slightly less-complex passage and then complete a graphic organizer for which the key event and one cause and one effect have been provided. While the teacher meets with small groups during this phase to provide targeted supports to students in the areas of phonics, fluency, vocabulary, and comprehension (differentiated by the readiness levels of groups of students), she also checks on students' progress on these independently completed graphic organizers.

The deductive lesson design allows the teacher to explicitly model reading and reading comprehension along with how to identify and interpret cause and effect in text. The teacher has opportunities to provide immediate and specific corrective feedback, check for understanding, evaluate current levels of student proficiency, and differentiate instruction. Students have opportunities to observe and practice comprehending text and structured opportunities to practice and express themselves orally and in writing, and they receive targeted support based on their needs.

This lesson design represents a key aspect of RTI. Students receive high-quality, differentiated Tier 1 instruction in an essential skill—cause and effect. Based on each student's response to this level of support and to his or her performance in various practice opportunities, and based on the teacher's multiple opportunities to observe and assess student understanding, the teacher can, through collaboration with her grade-level team, identify students who may need supplemental support and the strategies that may be most successful.

The content, process, and product of such a lesson can be differentiated based on student readiness and need, and the lesson design can be used in kindergarten through third grade in any content area. In kindergarten, modifications may include oral or pictorial responses substituted for written responses. Moreover, phonemic awareness and phonics lessons work very well using such a design.

Inductive Lesson Design

A more inductive lesson design may be appropriate in certain settings, particularly when students and classes experience success with deductive lessons that follow a more traditional gradual release of responsibility format. One example of a more constructivist, inductive approach to instruction is the lesson design shown in figure 1.6. Deductive lesson design is a more explicit, direct instructional model that begins with the teacher modeling and then gradually releasing responsibility to students. The inductive lesson design presented in this section, while not purely constructivist, begins with student-led inquiry before the teacher begins facilitating and guiding the learning process. Both types of learning experiences have their place in classrooms.

Figure 1.6: Inductive lesson design.

What follows is a sample inductive lesson from second grade for which the standard (RL.2.3) is, "Describe how characters in a story respond to major events and challenges" from the Reading Standards for Literature in grade 2, and the objective is, "Students will be able to compare and contrast characters' responses to major events in a story to assist in making meaning of text" (NGA & CCSSO, 2010a).

You Do It Together

The inductive lesson design may begin with a shared, guided, or independent reading of the first portion of a story, perhaps the same story as in the previous example, *Make Way for Ducklings* (1941). In teams, students are asked to compare and contrast the ducklings' experiences in different parts of the city. The teacher encourages students to show their understanding in any way they feel is appropriate, and she posts the students' products in the classroom. Student teams then explain their products, with the teacher guiding student presentations.

Why Do It

Next, the teacher provides more context for the story—activating background knowledge, connecting the theme to other stories that the class has read, and providing visual supports for key vocabulary. The teacher then builds from the students' products and presentations to develop the concept of compare and contrast, perhaps culminating in the introduction of a graphic organizer to represent this comprehension skill. She then uses a topic familiar to students—meals at home versus meals at school—to introduce the graphic organizer, such as in figure 1.7 (page 30).

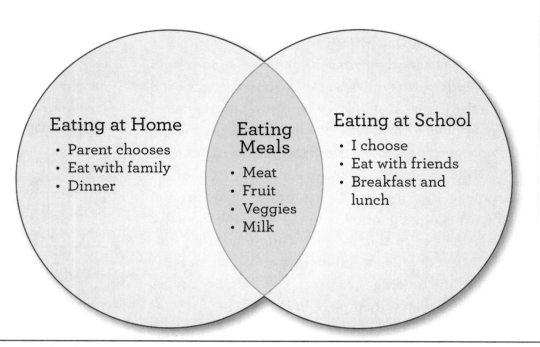

Figure 1.7: Sample of compare-and-contrast graphic organizer.

I Do It

Next, the teacher reads aloud a section of *Make Way for Ducklings*, metacognitively modeling her application of the comprehension skill (compare and contrast) and connecting her analyses both to the students' products and thinking and to the graphic organizer that she has introduced, while also interpreting the meaning of the passage.

We Do It Together

Following the explicit metacognitive teacher modeling, the teacher and the class read another section of the story together. Using think-pair-share strategies, the teacher elicits students' comparisons of key topics within a preidentified section. Students have numerous opportunities to think and express themselves. The teacher has numerous opportunities to hear student responses, providing immediate and specific corrective feedback in a timely manner and checking for understanding to determine the appropriate pace of the lesson.

You Do It Alone

Based on an evaluation of student performance during the You Do It Together phase that opened the lesson and the We Do It Together phase, the teacher assigns each student to a different group (color coded) for independent practice, as described in the earlier deductive cause-and-effect lesson sample. Tasks are differentiated for student readiness levels and needs. The students also complete a compare-and-contrast product of their choosing for the next section of the story. While the teacher meets with small groups during this phase to provide targeted support to students, she also checks on students' progress on the compare-and-contrast tasks, perhaps first meeting with the students about whom she is most concerned to ensure they begin their analysis well before providing them with targeted supports in phonics, fluency, vocabulary, or comprehension.

While more-inductive lessons such as this have structures, routines, and a predictable flow that are similar to deductive lessons, they allow for more student inquiry early in the lesson and give students the opportunity to construct their own meaning. Inductive lessons must have a place in a teacher's repertoire and may be most appropriate once the teacher and students gain comfort and confidence with deductive lessons or during the second and third days on a given topic (after a more-deductive lesson day).

To support teachers in improving their instructional craft, lesson studies are among the most effective and inexpensive forms of professional development (Stigler & Hiebert, 1999); the co-creation and co-implementation of deductive and inductive lessons is an appropriate and effective focus for professional development in instructional planning.

Making Time for Reading

In addition to using the gradual release of responsibility model that includes both deductive and inductive lessons, teachers must give students time to read in school. The most effective classrooms both explicitly teach comprehension skills and provide time for students to apply those skills in authentic settings when reading books of their choosing within their appropriate range. Richard Allington and Rachael Gabriel (2012) describe what can be incredibly powerful, important, and low-cost elements of every K–3 classroom:

- **Every child reads something he or she chooses**—Students must have access to many books and a choice of what to read, in addition to teacher-led or teacher-directed readings.

- **Every child reads accurately**—Students need guidance on choosing books at their level that they can read with 98 percent accuracy. Easy reading makes reading easy.

- **Every child reads something he or she understands**—Making meaning is the goal of reading. Too often, struggling readers receive support only with isolated skills. Exemplary teachers differentiate instruction so that all students read books accurately, fluently, and with understanding.

- **Every child talks with peers about reading**—Conversations with peers improve students' comprehension and engagement. Students should be asked to analyze, comment on, compare, think about, and talk about what they've read with a classmate. Struggling readers are not given this opportunity as often.

- **Every child listens to a fluent adult read aloud**—Listening to a teacher model fluency and comprehension improves many aspects of a student's reading: vocabulary, background knowledge, sense of story, awareness of genre, text structure, and comprehension. Kindergarten through grade 3 teachers should regularly engage in this shared reading activity.

Reading Assessment

Before discussing how to monitor student proficiency and diagnose student needs, we must first examine the purpose of assessment, which includes grading. There are two troubling misunderstandings about assessment and grading within schools (Marzano, 2006). The first misunderstanding is that instruction is distinct from assessment. For example, "I taught the content for a week, and then I gave the students a test." There is an unfortunate reluctance to assess students during the course of instruction, perhaps because teachers feel that they are unqualified to craft a valid assessment and that informal evidence gathered during the course of instruction is unreliable and invalid to inform teaching and impossible to use when assigning grades. This is simply not the case. The second misunderstanding follows from the first: assessing for instruction and assessing for the purpose of determining a grade are distinct. In fact, assessment is assessment, and the information gathered during assessment can be used for a variety of important purposes.

With one or two exceptions (such as curriculum-based measurements [CBMs] and psychological testing), there is only one purpose for assessment: to inform future instruction. A single assessment can be summative or formative, used to diagnose or monitor progress, and used for universal screening or to provide information about current levels of performance. Grading is a way of communicating levels of performance at a specific point in time. To the extent that assessments (formal and informal) provide the evidence teachers use to assign grades, assessments and grading are indistinguishable.

For example, sixty-second oral reading fluency tests are used to universally screen or to check in with all students three times a year to determine whether or not they are on track in the area of reading. They can be used to validly and reliably monitor student progress and to formatively inform the pace and content of instruction for individuals and groups of students. They can be used diagnostically, by conducting an error analysis, to determine specific student needs. Oral reading fluency tests can be used to determine current levels of performance and summatively to record student performance and communicate it to stakeholders.

Grades are often viewed as a referendum on teaching or teachers or a permanent judgment of students. This should not be the case. Rather, they should provide information about how students are performing at a specific moment in time as measured against a predetermined, precommunicated standard. From its inception with the publication of *A Nation at Risk* (National Commission on Excellence in Education, 1983), standards-based education reform was designed—at least in part—to minimize the ways in which grading distracts from teaching and learning. A common scale for standards-based grades is as follows:

> **1 = Below standard**—The student is not responding to instruction and intervention in relation to this standard.

> **2 = Approaching standard**—The student is responding to instruction and intervention in relation to this standard but has not yet met the standard.

> **3 = Meeting standard**—The student has met this standard.

> **4 = Exceeding standard**—The student has met this standard, exceeding the standard by demonstrating greater depth of knowledge or by demonstrating mastery at a more advanced level.

This form of standards-based grading implies a growth mindset rather than a fixed mindset (Dweck, 2006). Moreover, in standards-based grading, students' current levels of understanding and mastery are determined to be at a 1, 2, 3, or 4 level. In contrast, letter grades are almost always determined based on numerical averages of multiple assignments.

In addition to the scale, teachers must also understand what it looks like when a student has met the standard. Without detailed and consistently applied knowledge of what meeting the standard looks like, grading will continue to create anxiety and will continue to distract. I recommend that teachers collaboratively determine what meeting the standard looks like. Buffum, Mattos, and Weber (2011) recommend a tool called the essential standards chart, which is described later in the chapter (page 36).

Diagnosing Reading Needs

When assessments or grades determine that a student needs supplemental supports in reading or when a student does not respond to initial, high-quality instruction and initial intervention, teachers should take steps to diagnose specific areas of need. An effective, efficient, and free way of diagnosing student needs is to listen to a student read and respond while analyzing patterns of errors. This can be done as students identify initial sounds, identify letter names, segment or omit phonemes, blend consonants and vowels, or respond to questions designed to assess their comprehension. Teachers must trust their professional judgment to make these diagnoses. The Reading Domains, Skills, and Assessments document (page 154–155) included in the appendix section of the book will help guide this diagnostic process. In addition, there are relatively inexpensive tools that schools can use to diagnose reading needs, such as CORE: Assessing Reading (Consortium on Reading Excellence, 2008) and the Qualitative Reading Inventory 5 (Leslie & Caldwell, 2011). The CORE resource provides over a dozen validated diagnostic tools. The Qualitative Reading

Inventory 5 allows teachers to determine where reading needs may exist as students interact in prereading, reading, and postreading tasks on six passages per level, from preprimer and up.

It is not the act of diagnosing that benefits student learning, of course; it's what we do with the information. RTI is a fantastic philosophy, framework, and orientation to adopt when committing to and ensuring that all students learn at very high levels. But teachers who simply go through the motions of RTI will not succeed. RTI is only successful when implemented with intensity, a sense of urgency, and the expectation that, with time, all students will learn at very high levels.

With RTI, teachers diagnose so that they know what to prescribe. In other words, teachers administer diagnostic assessments (or use data, information, and evidence from assessments to diagnose) in order to determine immediate, targeted next steps. Used diagnostically, nearly any assessment will allow educators to determine where there is a breakdown in reading development. It's not recommended that all students receive these lengthy assessments. That is inefficient, unnecessary, may result in teachers becoming resentful of the tests, and can lead to misuse. The collaborative manner in which we use assessment data is more important than the assessment itself.

The key to success with RTI is in the school's response when students are not succeeding, even after receiving high-quality instruction. Teachers must respond early, with intensity, and diagnostically so that students can, as quickly as possible, begin reading for meaning. Educators must build in the structures, such as those associated with RTI systems of support, to diagnose the specific needs of students who do not respond to instruction and intervention. Then, schools must carve out time to provide supplemental supports that are in addition to core, Tier 1 instruction.

It is important to remember that if it's predictable, it's preventable. Educators can predict that a few students will have difficulty acquiring and mastering reading. They can prevent the negative impact of these early difficulties with appropriate interventions.

Monitoring Reading Progress

The reauthorization of the Individuals with Disabilities Education Act (U.S. Department of Education, 2004a) encourages schools to intervene early. It also allows schools to determine eligibility for special education with a diagnosis of specific learning disability if students do not respond to high-quality intervention. If a student truly has a learning disability, early intervention will make it more likely that educators can determine supports that will benefit the student and less likely his or her difficulties will become entrenched, leading to failure. The discrepancy model, also known as the "wait-to-fail model," is often used to determine eligibility for special education services in third grade or later because only then would a sufficiently large discrepancy between IQ and achievement have developed. This model can be avoided if there is early intervention and monitoring from kindergarten to grade 3.

The monitoring tools on pages 154–155 of the appendix are a powerful and efficient way to monitor student progress. Educators should always monitor progress using multiple measures, including observations and evidence of performance over time. These multiple measures should include a CBM (special tests given every one to two weeks to students who are at risk) that have the following important attributes:

- They are sensitive to small improvement.
- They are valid and reliable across multiple administrations and with several alternate versions.
- They are brief and typically timed, and they measure automaticity.
- They assess specific skills within a broader domain. For example, a nonsense or pseudoword decoding measure is designed to assess a student's current level of understanding, as well as progress, within the domain of early phonics.
- They allow for a comparison between a student's most recent performance and past performance, as well as a comparison between a student's performance across multiple assessments and a norm-referenced goal.

Many reading CBMs are free and designed to do the following:

- Ensure that teachers are providing the most appropriate supports for students.
- Validate the effectiveness of instruction and supplemental interventions.
- Give confidence to students as they view their progress over time.
- Increase teachers' sense of self-efficacy as they help students plot their progress over time.

There are, however, a few notes of caution regarding progress monitoring using CBMs. First, teachers must ensure that they are using the CBM that most closely matches students' areas of need and the corresponding instructional supports. For example, if a second-grade student's difficulties are not based on a lack of skill but rather on a lack of will (such as a lack of organization or motivation), then progress monitoring using an oral reading fluency CBM is not the best choice. A better choice would be to use check-in/check-out (CICO) procedures that supply information about the student's response to the behavioral supports that the teacher and school provide. While not a pure CBM, CICO is an appropriate, informative way to monitor behavior. Likewise, if a second-grade student's skills in the area of phonics are found to be lacking (not in the areas of fluency or comprehension), then an oral reading fluency CBM is not the best choice. Rather, a CBM that assesses phonics, such as a nonsense word (or pseudoword) fluency assessment, would provide information to validate this student's progress.

Progress monitoring can be a positive addition; it's fulfilling to frequently check in on the progress of a student and observe the results of hard work. Teachers should share progress as measured by CBMs with students so students can set goals for their future performance. It is important to remember that progress in a specific skill as measured by a CBM does not indicate that a student has achieved success in reading; rather, it is a means to an end—the goal is that the student makes meaning of text in natural, authentic settings.

Designing Reading Units of Instruction

A scope and sequence of instruction (figure 1.1, page 18, and at **go.solution-tree.com/rti**) is a general curriculum map that represents a proposed order of reading skills through each month of kindergarten, first grade, second grade, and third grade. Teams of teachers should design curriculum maps for themselves. Two tools can assist teams in this work (Buffum et al., 2012): the essential standards chart and the teaching-assessing cycle.

The Essential Standards Chart

An essential standards chart (see figure 1.8) guides teams through the unpacking of essential standards. (Completed examples of essential standards charts are available online at **go.solution -tree.com/rti**.) Teams first collaboratively identify the most essential standards in their grade level. These are the must-know standards—the standards that have endurance, leverage, and readiness (Reeves, 2002). Not all standards can be essential. Once teams have identified the essentials, they use the chart to translate the standard into student-friendly language and ensure that the standard actually represents a specific learning target. Standards are often written in "educationeze" and not readily understood by students, parents, and even teachers. Simplifying the language of the standard will contribute to a clearer understanding of what needs to be learned. Standards often are broadly written so that they actually represent several distinct learning targets. When teams define standards more specifically, teachers can provide more targeted instruction and more accurately assess student mastery. Thus, standards should be converted to learning targets—a standard that has been more specifically defined.

The second column of the chart guides teams through the unpacking process. In order to fully understand, define, teach, and assess the standard, teachers must have a common understanding of what mastery of the standard looks like. What type of question will students successfully answer to demonstrate mastery? What task could they complete to show mastery of the standard? What product or work could students complete to show mastery? This process will not only more fully define the standard, it will also clarify the desired outcome of instruction among all teachers in the team, thus ensuring a guaranteed and viable curriculum for all students (Marzano, 2003); provide items for common formative assessments; and aid in the process of planning instruction. The essential standards chart also guides teams to identify prerequisite skills during the process of planning for instruction. With this knowledge, teams of teachers could potentially provide preteaching to groups of students who lack prerequisite knowledge or skills, thereby making success more possible.

What Is It We Expect Students to Learn?					
Grade:	Subject:	Semester:	Team Members:		
Description of Standard	**Example of Rigor**	**Prerequisite Skills**	**When Taught?**	**Common Summative Assessment**	**Extension Standards**
What is the essential standard to be learned? Describe in student-friendly vocabulary.	What does proficient student work look like? Provide an example or description.	What prior knowledge, skills, or vocabulary are needed for a student to master this standard?	When will this standard be taught?	What assessment(s) will be used to measure student mastery?	What will we do when students have already learned this standard?

1. **Endurance:** Will this standard provide students with knowledge and skills that are valuable beyond a single test date?
2. **Leverage:** Will it provide knowledge and skills that are valuable in multiple disciplines?
3. **Readiness:** Will it provide students with knowledge and skills essential for success in the next grade/level of instruction?

Figure 1.8: Essential standards chart.

Source: Reeves, 2002. Reprinted from Buffum, Mattos, & Weber, 2012.

As teams complete the chart, they should determine when the essential standards will be taught, thus contributing to a fluid and comprehensive curriculum map. Additionally, teams should agree about when and how frequently they will administer and analyze results from common formative assessments. These assessments can be built from the types of items identified in the second column of the essential standards chart. The last column of the chart guides teams in identifying and crafting enrichment tasks with greater depth and complexity for students who have mastered the learning, instead of simply assigning them more work or work from the next grade level.

Completing the essential standards chart is a foundational task for teacher teams. It should be one of the first orders of business for teams and may take months or even years. It is most definitely crucial work and time well spent. When used with the team teaching-assessing cycle, the essential standards chart helps both operationalize RTI and lead to higher levels of learning for a greater number of students.

The Teaching-Assessing Cycle

The teaching-assessing cycle (figure 1.9) offers one way in which teachers can plan to support all students during a unit. Teams begin at the top of the cycle, completing the essential standards chart, selecting and unwrapping or unpacking essentials for the upcoming unit. They then assess prerequisite skills and provide preteaching. Consider the following scenario.

A new unit of instruction in second grade is scheduled to commence in a week. The team of three teachers uses tickets out the door or exit slips to conclude the last several lessons of the preceding unit. These tickets or exit slips contain questions that assess student knowledge of prerequisite skills that are necessary for the next unit. After quickly identifying who does and does not possess prerequisite knowledge, the team of teachers sets aside a day after the end of the preceding unit and before the beginning of the following unit to preteach prerequisite skills to students in need. One teacher accepts responsibility for completing this task with students from all three classes. Meanwhile, the other two teachers complete extension activities with the remaining students—extension activities that have been previously planned through the completion of the essential standards chart. While the needs of all students lacking prerequisite skills will certainly not be met, this preteaching is a proactive response that will make a positive difference.

Differentiated, personalized, and unique instruction then begins in the three classrooms, with teachers administering and analyzing previously agreed-upon common formative assessments at agreed-upon dates. As the bottom of the cycle indicates, teachers use their analyses of the assessments to modify instruction for the remainder of the unit and to provide remediation to students who have been identified as struggling midway through the unit and enrichment and extension to others. This is done similar to the manner in which prerequisite instruction was given before the unit began, with one teacher providing remedial support and the other two extension.

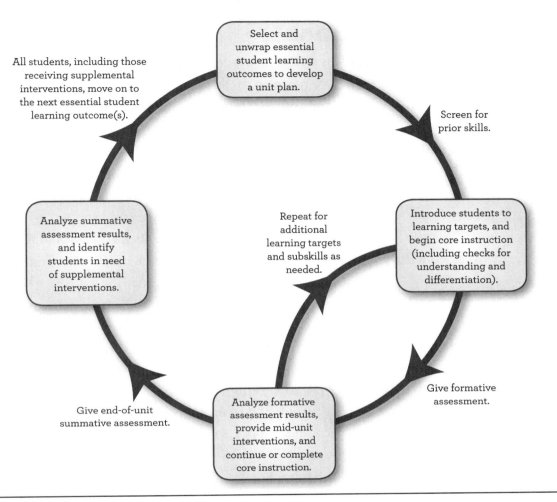

Figure 1.9: The teaching-assessing cycle.

Source: Reprinted from Buffum, Mattos, & Weber, 2012.

The unit of instruction continues, and at the agreed-upon date, teachers give an end-of-unit assessment. While this assessment is then followed by a repetition of the cycle that addresses a new set of essential standards, students who have yet to master essentials are not forgotten. As indicated in the diagram, schoolwide teams, made up of administrators, specialists, and clinicians, and the teacher teams identify when these students will continue to receive support for the just-completed unit while the entire class (teachers and the rest of the students) begins the next unit.

Both the essential standards chart and the teaching-assessing cycle apply to all content areas. The samples of essential standards at **go.solution-tree.com/rti** show examples from writing, mathematics, and English language, in addition to reading.

Reading Interventions

If core instruction is not resulting in adequate student learning, teachers must be prepared to intervene with the time, space, personnel, and materials to provide support. Educators will understandably ask about the necessary or optimal frequency and duration of supports to provide to students at risk. While students will likely respond to intervention at a rate that will significantly close the gap in thirty minutes of daily intensive and targeted support, some experts suggest that only two months of additional progress can be gained through this level of support and that ninety minutes of daily supports are necessary to adequately close the gap (Allington, 2009). We can predict that some students will require even more additional time and support to learn at the high levels expected for all students. To make certain that all students have access to the time and support they require, educators must determine the when, who, and what of intervention.

When Should Schools Complete Interventions?

Perhaps the biggest challenge that teachers, teams, and schools face is determining when they should provide supplemental supports. While before- and after-school options may be considered, research and practice demonstrate that they are not optimally or universally effective (Halpern, 1999; Kane, 2004; Posner & Vandell, 1994). In addition, students cannot typically be required to attend, additional personnel costs are required, and offering five-day-a-week intervention before and after school is rare. Let's assume, then, that supports will be provided during the instructional day. Time is the most precious of resources in schools; many educators wonder when they can provide supplemental support during the school day.

The first and best option is to provide supplemental small-group support during the reading block for students who have similar needs. Whether this block of time is known as centers, stations, workshop, or universal access time, kindergarten through third-grade teachers should structure time within the reading block (and the writing and mathematics block), when instruction can be differentiated for struggling learners. While the teacher meets with small groups of students, the other students in the class have the opportunity to work independently on tasks of an appropriate level. Those tasks will most likely not be the same; they will be differentiated based on student readiness. Students can successfully work independently when teachers establish routines, set expectations for student behavior, and frequently reinforce and review procedures, which allow the teacher to provide support to small groups. There are several resources that outline how a teacher creates the environment (the routines, procedures, and expectations) for independent work to take place (Fountas & Pinnell, 1996; Tomlinson, 1999, 2001). They all have this in common: creating these environments takes time, the process to full implementation will be gradual, and teachers must continuously model, practice, and reinforce expectations.

When students can successfully work independently, the teacher can meet with small groups of students. There are four main categories of support the teacher can provide during these sessions:

1. **Reteaching**—The teacher provides a second opportunity for a group of students to access the day's or week's key content, with the chance for more frequent interactions with students and more immediate diagnoses and corrective feedback.

2. **Preteaching**—The teacher anticipates that a group of students may have difficulty with an upcoming lesson and provides background knowledge and a preview of concepts or a review of key prerequisite knowledge.

3. **Remediation**—The teacher systematically fills significant gaps that may exist in key knowledge. While similar to reteaching, remediation will likely be a longer-term project that focuses on knowledge that most students in a given grade level would have possessed prior to the beginning of the unit or the beginning of the school year.

4. **Extension**—The teacher provides more depth and complexity of content and concepts for students who have already demonstrated an adequate level of mastery.

Every student should have the opportunity to meet with the teacher in a small group. The focus of the meeting will depend on the student's readiness levels and needs. In an effective use of human resources, some schools have had success using additional staff members during this small-group time. Whether paraprofessionals, special education teachers, or reading specialists, these additional staff members provide another resource for small-group work. Students who are most at risk may meet with both the classroom teacher and the additional staff member. Teacher teams must determine whether a second opportunity to meet with a teacher in a small group to receive supplemental support or working independently is most valuable for a student. There is not an unlimited amount of time during the instructional day during which students can receive supplemental supports—students will miss something, at least for a period of time. However, reading (and writing and number sense) are such critical skills that if deficiencies are not addressed with a sense of urgency in the early grades, students will suffer from lasting and dramatic negative effects (Adams, 1990; Coyne & Harn, 2006; Coyne, Kame'enui, & Simmons, 2004; Dickinson & Neuman, 2006; Duncan et al., 2007).

If students still do not demonstrate mastery after differentiated whole-group instruction and with supplemental supports in small groups, schools must provide additional interventions. These interventions should not be in place of core instruction in reading, writing, or mathematics; however, they usually must be provided in place of other new content. The decision about what content students miss to receive interventions is difficult and should be made by teacher teams. While students will miss content, they need not miss the same content every day or week. For example, following are two options:

1. Often, specials or electives are scheduled throughout the week, with perhaps library time on Mondays and Wednesdays from 9:00–9:30 and computer time on Tuesdays and Thursdays from 10:00–10:30. If a reading intervention is scheduled for

struggling students each Monday and Wednesday from 9:00–9:30, they will miss library time every week. However, if the period during which library time and computer time are switched each week, then the negative impact of missing these important opportunities is reduced. Or perhaps a reading intervention is scheduled from 1:00–1:30, the time during which social studies instruction occurs. Perhaps science instruction occurs from 1:30–2:00. If the time slot for social studies and science is swapped each week while the time for reading intervention remains fixed, students in need of reading intervention will not miss the same critical subject for an extended period of time. There will be implications for teachers as they plan their units of instruction, but the payoff for students is great.

2. Some schools have built an intervention block into their daily schedule. During this block, students are more homogeneously grouped based on their needs. Students who require intervention support receive this assistance in a small group, and there is an added benefit: other students who would benefit from daily differentiated instruction, perhaps extension or enrichment in a content area, have the time within the day to receive it.

Who Should Provide Interventions?

In many elementary schools, human resources are not optimally used to provide direct academic supports to students. Schools should inventory their available human resources to ensure that personnel are scheduled and assigned so that they can best support students. This may mean staggering the times during which half-day instructional aides work. It will probably also mean that auxiliary staff members are scheduled and assigned by the administrators or a schoolwide RTI team rather than by grade levels or individual teachers, as is sometimes the case. Given the expectations for student success, educators cannot afford to waste the time and talents of any staff member.

Many schools have specialists on their campus—special educators, reading specialists, bilingual lead teachers, or interventionists. While they may have primary tasks that they are required to complete, in a school that accepts collective responsibility (Buffum et al., 2012) for all students' learning, they should have time within their day scheduled to meet the learning needs of all students—even if they are not identified with a label such as special education, English learner, dyslexic, or ADD. While these specialists have specialized training that qualifies them to provide specific, targeted, and intensive supports to particular groups of students, they are usually qualified to support students with other needs.

Paraprofessionals can also provide supplemental supports. The No Child Left Behind Act (2002) specifies that paraprofessionals be highly qualified (along with other teaching staff). All staff can be highly effective if administrators provide them with initial and ongoing professional development in pedagogy, in the content areas they are supporting, and in the programs they are using, including how to work collaboratively to make instructional and curricular decisions.

Classroom teachers should be providing supplemental supports to students who are at risk in reading. Classroom teachers from kindergarten through third grade are the best staff members to provide initial and supplemental support to these students since they know them and the content best. While their instructional days should be spent providing differentiated supports to both the whole class and small groups of their students in multiple subject areas, they may be able to provide supplemental Tier 2 and 3 supports as well. In the spirit of collective responsibility and with the understanding that reading is preeminently important for students, a teacher within a grade level may provide supplemental supports in reading while colleagues and the other students within that grade level teach and learn social studies, science, or other content areas. For example, one teacher within a grade level with four total teachers and one hundred total students could provide support to students who are at risk in reading while the other teachers and students engage in teaching and learning in other content areas. If there were ten students at risk, this would leave ninety students to be divided among the remaining three teachers, with thirty students per teacher. Similarly creative uses of staff could provide vital instruction to students in need of supplemental support.

What Resources Should Be Used?

After addressing when to provide additional supports and who should provide those supports, the last consideration is what materials and resources teachers should use. Educators may wonder if they should use free, low-cost, or teacher-created materials, or if the school should purchase commercially available intervention programs. Teachers possess the knowledge to select, craft, and teach interventions. However, teachers have full-time jobs of some importance—they teach students. When do they have the time to design appropriately scoped and sequenced intervention programs? Moreover, classroom teachers are not always the staff members serving as interventionists. While many interventionists are educators who understand sound pedagogy, others may be newer teachers, paraprofessionals, or even volunteers. Well-designed lessons within commercially available programs provide a foundation for successful, differentiated intervention, as long as they are differentiated based on student need. The following are some guidelines for what to look for in a purchased intervention program:

- **Consider quality**—The Florida Center for Reading Research (2011) and the Oregon Reading First Center (2011), among other centers, provide resources to assist in evaluating programs and have also rated programs.

- **Consider cost**—There can be broad differences between two teacher-based or pencil-and-paper (as opposed to technologically based) interventions that are quite similar in completeness and quality. While one might argue that you get what you pay for, some of the very best commercially available interventions are relative bargains. For example, a cost comparison of two intervention programs reviewed by the Florida Center for Reading Research (2011) with equal quality ratings revealed one solution with a cost five times as high as the other. In addition, it's important to remember that in large part, it's the teacher who makes the program effective.

- **Ensure the program is systematic and explicit**—Look for programs that have well-defined, well-designed, well-described, and logically scoped and sequenced lessons. These free up teacher time for teaching and moreover, interventionists with a broad range of experiences can successfully implement such programs.

- **Consider training**—Does the program offer professional development? If so, what is the quality, and how complex is the program to implement? No matter how well designed a program, no intervention is foolproof. The most significant factor in any educational endeavor, including interventions, is the quality of the educators (DuFour & Marzano, 2011).

- **Consider embedded assessments**—Schools may elect to use their own assessments to identify students for a particular intervention, to determine which portions of the program are appropriate, and to monitor the progress of students and the efficacy of the program. Assessments that are embedded within programs are internal validations of student progress, and schools should also externally validate student progress using assessments such as CBMs. Nonetheless, the assessments embedded within commercially available interventions can be useful, and if a school decides that they will be the primary tool for placement and monitoring, they must be carefully examined.

- **Consider technology**—A few focused and effective web- or software-based programs exist. However, these programs are often prohibitively expensive and overly broad in scope. Moreover, software requires hardware, and hardware has a limited lifespan. Schools should consider these costs. The increased use of tablet devices and application-based software may lower costs and increase the specificity of technological supports.

The goal when selecting resources, whether teacher created or commercially available, should be to ensure that teachers and students use the best possible materials.

The Four Questions of RTI in Reading

Teacher teams and schoolwide teams should regularly consider the following four questions when determining whether students are responding to instruction and intervention (Buffum et al., 2012):

1. **About which students do we have concerns?** There are free, efficient, and validated reading screeners that immediately and frequently identify students who may need differentiated or supplemental supports.

2. **In what areas do we have concerns?** Error analyses of students' responses on reading screeners can help staff diagnose problems. There are low-cost diagnostic assessments that teachers can use to help further target reading supports for students who do not respond to instruction and interventions.

3. **What are we currently doing to support the student and meet the student's needs? What supports will be provided in the future?** There are free resources, strategies, and information on high-quality commercially available programs that should help staff ameliorate virtually any deficiency for a K–3 student who is at risk.

4. **Has the student responded to the instruction and interventions (the supports) that we have been providing?** There are free, efficient, and validated curriculum-based measurements that staffs can use to monitor the progress of students who struggle with reading.

Summary

Educators in kindergarten through third grade need a clear definition and understanding of what students need to learn in reading. Research supports the fact that students should receive explicit supports in all domains of reading before kindergarten and through the elementary grades (Adams, 1990; Bowman et al., 2000; Coyne & Harn, 2006; Coyne et al., 2004; Dickinson & Neuman, 2006). Assessment, frequent checking for understanding, and immediate corrective feedback must be seamlessly connected to instruction, and teacher knowledge of student performance must inform instruction on a minute-by-minute, day-by-day, and unit-by-unit basis. In addition, teachers must design and use interventions (assessments) to address the needs of students who struggle (Buffum et al., 2012). Educators must provide those supports with intensity, a sense of urgency, and with the expectation that they can support every student so that he or she can achieve a high level of learning. Use the reproducible Guiding Goals for K–3 Reading checklist (page 46) to help determine the next steps you will take in your (classroom, team, school, or district) RTI-based reading program.

The next chapter will focus on research, content, instruction, assessment, and intervention in writing—the companion subject to reading. There are several sound approaches to teaching writing, and our expectations for the writing of students in kindergarten through third grade should be high.

Guiding Goals for K–3 Reading

Goal	Long-Term Vision	First Steps
Fully understand the five domains of reading	Staff can articulate the ins and outs of phonological awareness, phonics, fluency, vocabulary, and comprehension. Staff can integrate explicit instruction and authentic reading for meaning into lessons. Staff can diagnose student needs and prescribe immediate supports.	☐ All staff members engage in collaborative study of the domains, perhaps by reviewing the findings of the National Reading Panel or other balanced resources. ☐ Each staff member identifies and shares one key strategy for reinforcing each of the five domains.
Achieve consistency in diagnosing reading needs	Staff will collaboratively analyze student needs in order to differentiate supports.	☐ All staff rediscover running records and agree on a consistent way of recording errors, whether students are reading connected text or isolated phonemes, so that evidence of student need can be seamlessly and collaboratively discussed. ☐ Teacher teams set aside weekly time to collaboratively diagnose the reading needs of individual students.
Scope and sequence standards	Staff identifies the essential learning for reading, unpacks these essentials, and determines ways of assessing mastery.	☐ Staff collaboratively dialogues about existing state and Common Core State Standards. ☐ Teacher teams determine essential standards using research-based tools and protocols. ☐ Teams unpack essentials using the essential standards chart.
Organize instructional units	Teacher teams collaboratively design units of reading instruction and come to consensus regarding key content and common formative assessments.	☐ Teacher teams determine when units of instruction will occur. ☐ Team members agree on which essential standards they will address in each unit.

Organize instructional units *(continued)*		☐ Team members design common formative assessments and schedule when they will collaboratively analyze results. ☐ Team members plan in advance when they can provide preventative, proactive supports before, during, and after each unit.
Refine and study effective lessons, structures, and strategies.	Teacher teams collaboratively strive to improve their teaching, including how to best structure lessons.	☐ Teachers share ideas and routines that support the differentiation of content, process, and product. ☐ Teachers ensure that time for small-group learning is included in lessons. ☐ Teams plan on regular (at least quarterly) lesson studies in which teachers co-plan, co-teach, and co-review lessons in one another's classroom.
Identify interventions and progress-monitoring tools	Teacher teams investigate and share best practices in supporting students in the five domains of reading and agree on a tool and timeline for monitoring progress.	☐ Teachers regularly share strategies from print and Internet resources that are simple to implement and that have been shown to increase student learning. ☐ The staff identifies an efficient progress-assessment tool to quickly and accurately monitor student progress and inform learning. ☐ Teachers agree on which staff member will be responsible for monitoring progress as well as how often he or she will monitor progress and how often it will be analyzed collaboratively.

RTI in the Early Grades © 2013 Solution Tree Press • solution-tree.com
Visit **go.solution-tree.com/rti** to download this page.

CHAPTER 2

Writing

Writing, the art of communicating thoughts to the mind through the eye, is the great invention of the world.

ABRAHAM LINCOLN

The term *90/90/90 schools* is probably familiar to most educators; this idea, and the research behind it, has been transformative for education. In 90/90/90 schools, 90 percent of students come from ethnic minorities, 90 percent qualify for free or reduced-price lunch, and 90 percent meet state standards in reading and math. In his findings on 90/90/90 schools, Doug Reeves (2000) reminds us of both our moral imperative and the unlimited capacity of all children to learn at the very highest levels; neither socioeconomic nor linguistic nor ethnic characteristics need have any negative impact on student success. Through his work, Reeves also identified the five core principles of 90/90/90 schools:

1. A focus on academic achievement
2. Clear curriculum choices
3. Frequent assessment of student progress and multiple opportunities for improvement
4. An emphasis on writing
5. External scoring

The fourth element, "An emphasis on writing," will help frame this chapter.

Reeves notes that "by far, the most common characteristic of the '90/90/90 Schools' was their emphasis on requiring written responses in performance assessments" (2000, p. 190). Great schools—schools in which almost all students demonstrate significant academic growth—focus on writing, and specifically, on informational writing. Why does a focus on writing lead to gains across other domains and content areas, as Reeves found? Reeves deduced that writing helps both teachers and students: teachers' analyses of student writing yields a rich reservoir of information about student needs, and when students are required to write, they are required to organize their thinking more clearly as they communicate their solutions to problems. Writing is the ultimate literacy skill. Students develop other literacy skills, such as decoding, encoding, vocabulary, and comprehension, as they learn to write and write well. When student writing improves, it implies that other areas of literacy are also improving (Graham & Hebert, 2010; Graham & Perin, 2007; Harris, 2006; Reeves, 2000).

Reeves found that the best schools focused on informational writing. For example, research supports that students' writing of summaries is one of the most high-leverage types of writing they can engage in, a task that directly supports improved comprehension (Marzano et al., 2001).

Research on Early Writing

In *Writing to Read*, Steve Graham and Michael Hebert (2010) reviewed hundreds of studies on reading, writing, and the impacts of writing on reading. The report gives three recommendations for teachers and schools to follow in improving student writing and reading:

1. Students should write about what they read, including personal reactions and summaries. They should take structured notes and create and answer questions. This improves comprehension.

2. Students should receive explicit instruction in the writing process, the structures of effective writing, and the construction of sound sentences and paragraphs. This improves reading skills and comprehension.

3. Students should write as much as possible. Comprehension improves as the amount that students write increases.

In *Writing Next*, Graham and Dolores Perin (2007) make similar recommendations, suggesting that educators should:

- Analyze effective writing with students to guide student writing

- Provide a specific purpose and audience for writing

- Facilitate collaborative writing processes in which students prewrite, draft, revise, and edit

- Guide students through a writing process or writer's workshop approach

- Explicitly teach prewriting to guide students in generating and organizing ideas

- Explicitly teach students strategies for planning, revising, and editing

- Explicitly and systematically teach students to summarize

- Explicitly teach students to combine sentences and construct more complex sentences

- Engage students in an inquiry and analysis of content about which they will write

- Use writing, and expect students to use writing, as a tool for information processing and learning in all content areas

These recommendations should inform teaching methods to help students in kindergarten through third grade write well.

Key Writing Content

The CCSS provide a consistent, clear understanding of the content students are expected to learn at each grade level. The CCSS in kindergarten through third grade in the area of writing match the research recommendations. Table 2.1 (page 52) summarizes the standards.

What conclusions can be drawn from an analysis of the CCSS in the area of writing? First, seeing the standards summarized in table form reveals only subtle differences from grade to grade. The differences are slight and in the area of rigor, not necessarily in content. This is significant because it may allow for greater focus and continuity of content from year to year. There is also a lack of specificity or details in the standards. This highlights the importance of teachers unpacking standards—whether they are state standards, district power standards, or the CCSS (see Reeves, 2002, and Ainsworth, 2003a; 2003b). It is also important to note that, based on kindergarteners' unbounded capacity to produce authentic and creative writing, the CCSS may represent a slightly lower level of expectations than is appropriate.

The CCSS make it clear that key content in writing should include writing in three major genres: opinionative, informative, and narrative. Students should also demonstrate proficiency in planning, revising, and editing, as well as in using technology to produce and publish. Students should conduct research projects and organize information (for example, taking notes) that they glean from a variety of sources.

Table 2.2 (page 54) summarizes key content from the CCSS in written conventions. The CCSS for written conventions are clear and cumulative; third graders, for example, are expected to employ the correct conventions for third grade, as well as second grade, first grade, and kindergarten.

These standards for written conventions are incorporated in the analytic rubrics for each grade level that appear later in the chapter. The rubrics provide a starting point for teacher teams. They provide detail to the key content as suggested by the CCSS and can be used by teams in the instruction-assessment cycle.

Table 2.1: Synthesis of Common Core State Standards for Writing

Kindergarten	First Grade	Second Grade	Third Grade
Use a combination of drawing, dictating, and writing to compose opinion pieces that name the topic or title of the book and state an opinion or preference about the topic or book.	Write opinion pieces, introducing the topic or title of the book, stating an opinion, supplying reasons, and providing closure.	Write opinion pieces, introducing the topic or book, stating an opinion, supplying reasons, using linking words to connect opinions and reasons, and providing a concluding statement or section.	Write opinion pieces, supporting a point of view with reasons, using linking words and phrases, and providing a concluding statement.
Use a combination of drawing, dictating, and writing to compose informative texts that include the topic and information about the topic.	Write informative texts by naming a topic, supplying facts about the topic, and providing some sense of closure.	Write informative texts by introducing a topic, using facts and definitions to develop points, and providing a concluding statement or section.	Write informative texts to examine a topic and convey ideas and information clearly. Include illustrations, facts, definitions, and details; use linking words and phrases; and provide a concluding statement or section.
Use a combination of drawing, dictating, and writing to narrate an event or several events; sequence events; and provide a conclusion.	Write narratives recounting two or more sequenced events; include details; and provide some sense of closure.	Write narratives recounting a well-elaborated event or sequence of events; include details to describe actions, thoughts, and feelings; use temporal words to signal order; and provide a sense of closure.	Write narratives of real or imagined experiences, establishing a situation; introducing a narrator and characters; sequencing events; using dialogue; describing actions, thoughts, and feelings; and providing a sense of closure.
With guidance and support, respond to questions and suggestions from peers, and add details to strengthen writing.	With guidance and support, respond to questions and suggestions from peers, and add details to strengthen writing.	With guidance and support, strengthen writing by revising and editing.	With guidance and support, plan, revise, and edit.

With guidance and support, explore a variety of digital tools to produce and publish writing in collaboration with peers.	With guidance and support, use a variety of digital tools to produce and publish writing in collaboration with peers.	With guidance and support, use a variety of digital tools to produce and publish writing in collaboration with peers.	With guidance and support, use technology to produce and publish writing.
Participate in shared research and writing projects.	Participate in shared research and writing projects.	Participate in shared research and writing projects.	Conduct short research projects.
With guidance and support, recall information from experiences or gather information from provided sources to answer a question.	With guidance and support, recall information from experiences or gather information from provided sources to answer a question.	Recall information from experiences or gather information from provided sources to answer a question.	Recall information from experiences or gather information from print and digital sources, take notes on sources, and sort evidence into provided categories.
			Write both long-term (with time for research, reflection, and revision) and short-term pieces for a range of tasks, purposes, and audiences and within a variety of content areas.

Source: NGA & CCSSO, 2010a.

Table 2.2: Key Content in Language and Written Conventions

Kindergarten	First Grade	Second Grade	Third Grade
• Print upper- and lowercase letters.	• Print upper- and lowercase letters.	• Use collective nouns (such as *group*).	• Use nouns, pronouns, verbs, adjectives, and adverbs appropriately.
• Use nouns and verbs.	• Use common, proper, and possessive nouns.	• Use irregular plural nouns (such as *feet, children, teeth, mice, fish*).	• Use regular and irregular plural nouns.
• Form regular plural nouns by adding /s/ or /es/ (such as *dog, dogs; wish, wishes*).	• Use singular and plural nouns with matching verbs in basic sentences (such as *he hops, we hop*).	• Use reflexive pronouns (such as *myself, ourselves*).	• Use abstract nouns (such as *childhood*).
• Use question words (interrogatives) (such as *who, what, where, when, why, how*).	• Use personal, possessive, and indefinite pronouns (such as *I, me, my; they, them, their; anyone, everything*).	• Use the past tense of irregular verbs (such as *sat, hid, told*).	• Use regular and irregular verbs.
• Use prepositions (such as *to, from, in, out, on, off, for, of, by, with*).	• Use verbs to convey past, present, and future (such as *Yesterday I walked home; Today I walk home; Tomorrow I will walk home*).	• Use adjectives and adverbs appropriately.	• Use the simple verb tenses (such as *I walked; I walk; I will walk*).
	• Use adjectives.	• Produce, expand, and rearrange complete simple and compound sentences (such as, *The boy watched the movie; The little boy watched the movie; The action movie was watched by the little boy*).	• Ensure subject-verb and pronoun-antecedent agreement.
	• Use conjunctions (*and, but, or, so, because*).		• Use comparative and superlative adjectives and adverbs appropriately.
	• Use determiners (articles, demonstratives).		• Use coordinating and subordinating conjunctions.
	• Use prepositions (*during, beyond, toward*).		• Produce simple, compound, and complex sentences.

• Capitalize the first word in a sentence and the pronoun *I*. • Use end punctuation. • Write a letter or letters for most consonant and short-vowel sounds (phonemes). • Spell simple words phonetically.	• Capitalize dates and names of people. • Use end punctuation. • Use commas in dates and to separate single words in a series. • Use conventional spelling for words with common spelling patterns and for frequently occurring irregular words. • Spell untaught words phonetically.	• Capitalize holidays, product names, and geographic names. • Use commas in greetings and closings of letters. • Use an apostrophe to form contractions and frequently occurring possessives. • Generalize learned spelling patterns when writing words (such as *cage* → *badge; boy* → *boil*). • Consult reference materials, including beginning dictionaries, as needed to check and correct spellings.	• Capitalize appropriate words in titles. • Use commas in addresses and quotation marks in dialogue. • Use possessives. • Use conventional spelling for high-frequency words and for adding suffixes to base words (such as *sitting, smiled, cries, happiness*). • Use spelling patterns and generalizations (such as word families, position-based spellings, syllable patterns, ending rules, meaningful word parts) in writing words. • Consult reference materials, including beginning dictionaries, as needed to check and correct spellings.

Source: NGA & CCSSO, 2010a.

Writing Instruction

Students can begin to produce connected writing before kindergarten. The most significant and ubiquitous method for organizing writing instruction is known as the writing process (Emig, 1977; Flower & Hayes, 1981). The writing process model helps define the steps through which writers work: students start with prewriting, followed by drafting a first effort, before revising for content, editing for conventions, and publishing and sharing, although the steps are overlapping and recursive. Lucy Calkins's writer's workshop model (1986) also frames the writing process. The principles of *Write From the Beginning* (Buckner, 2000) help students (and teachers) turn blank pages into a piece of writing to be revised and edited. *Write From the Beginning* mini-lessons, as well as mini-lessons associated with the six traits of writing (Northwest Regional Educational Laboratory, 1999), also provide supports to teachers and students for revising and editing. The traits serve to guide teachers through specific attributes of writing: ideas, organization, voice, word choice, sentence fluency, and conventions.

A review of these different approaches to writing instruction reveals the following:

- These approaches to writing actually have much in common.
- The writer's workshop model and the six traits provide the greatest support in the revise, edit, and publish processes.
- *Write From the Beginning* and similar approaches provide teachers and students with the most structured guidance in the prewriting and drafting processes.

Regie Routman (2004) summarizes writing instruction in the following way:

> *Our students will learn to "do" all the necessary skills and a whole lot more if we shift our focus to meaningful teaching of writing and then teach the necessary skills to support that writing. (p. 142)*

Meaningful teaching of writing and writing conventions modeled by the teacher and embedded throughout the writing process are the focus of the remainder of this chapter. The purpose of explicitly teaching students the processes and structures for writing is to provide scaffolds for the more authentic, natural writing that we want students to become proficient in. These structures and processes will equip proficient students as they tackle unfamiliar territories; for students at risk, these scaffolds are timely and urgent life rafts, representing the differences between closing the gap and continuing to struggle while falling further behind.

Writing may be the most difficult single act to teach students to do well, but it may also be the most important single skill that students can learn. This chapter outlines an effective, proven method for helping students prewrite, draft, revise, edit, and publish in kindergarten through third grade in an authentic, creative, and proficient manner. It also connects the principles of RTI to writing. Writing is a universal skill (Buffum et al., 2012); when students experience difficulties in writing, educators must provide targeted, structured supports as soon as needs are identified or students will have serious challenges expressing their mastery of content in curricular areas.

Writing Instruction in Kindergarten

Unique and critical to kindergarten is the importance of drawing to the writing process. While teacher modeling is always critical and should be present in first through third grades, teacher modeling of writing and drawing is a fundamental part of kindergarten writing.

Teachers should model drawing and writing on a daily basis as a precursor to daily student writing. The teacher should first draw a picture that focuses on an opinionative, informative, or narrative prompt (the three genres identified in the CCSS). The teacher thinks aloud while drawing a picture that includes the following key attributes:

- Characters that are accurately represented with appropriate details
- Settings that are accurately represented with appropriate details
- Characters that are grounded or appropriately placed in the setting
- Colors that are appropriately used
- Items within the drawing that have reasonable functionality
- A drawing that tells the story of a single topic, event, or set of events

In other words, drawings should pictorially represent the type of high-quality writing that teachers expect from students.

The teacher then writes simple sentences with simple subjects and predicates that match the drawing. The teacher models how to spell phonetically and elicits suggestions from students. For example, when writing *spent*, as in "I spent the weekend with my family," the teacher may ask students to think about the first sounds they hear in *spent*. Then the teacher may ask the students—who are working in pairs—to tell one another the sounds they hear ("A partner, tell your B partner the first sounds you hear"). Next, the teacher may randomly call on a student to share the partner dialogue ("What sounds did you and your partner discuss? What letters would I use to write that?"). Similar interactive writing could be used to discuss medial and ending sounds, punctuation, and other elements of the sentences. While teachers may not use this level of student interaction for every sound and word, this think-pair-share process takes only thirty seconds and is a great way of engaging students.

After the teacher model, the class may collaboratively create a word bank based on the prompt before students create their own drawings and compose their own sentences like the teacher model. Some students may successfully complete an accurate illustration. Others may mimic the teacher model, with or without sentence frames to support their writing. Other students should be encouraged to write more originally from the prompt. These differentiation practices are essential at all grade levels. This model of a research-based, direct-instruction lesson design is representative of the same type of gradual release of responsibility lesson described in the previous chapter (Hattie, 2009).

Writing Instruction in Grades 1–3

The writing process should be an important part of kindergarten, but it begins in earnest in first grade. The modeling, scaffolds, and supports described in the following sections may be temporary for some students and are intended to move students toward authentic, independent writing that solidifies their success, confidence, and love for writing—the ultimate expression of literacy.

Prewriting

Before beginning the writing process, the teacher should explain the focus of the lesson. The teacher should then choose prompts connected to topics and content areas students are currently studying, and make these connections explicit. The teacher should read aloud fiction and nonfiction texts that match the theme or style represented by the prompt both before and during the writing process. Rubrics (detailed descriptions of the attributes of writing) can be used to analyze strengths and areas for improvement. Rubrics should be reviewed with students so that they understand the expectations and the ways in which their writing will be scored. Teachers should consider focusing on a few traits or a portion of the total rubric to help focus students' attention. Anchor papers—examples of writing that demonstrate a level of proficiency and can be used to identify specific and general attributes of quality work—can be incredibly useful tools in the writing process. Share any anchor papers that might be available, including actual student work from prior years or from other classrooms that represent a high level of writing. Use anchor papers and a rubric to show students what makes a piece of writing exceptional.

Next, teachers should introduce the prompt, identifying key words, an appropriate audience, and a meaningful purpose, thinking aloud and modeling for students so that they can eventually complete these tasks independently. To begin the organization and planning of the prewriting process, teachers should first model brainstorming for the prompt, perhaps using a graphic organizer. Figure 2.1 shows an example of brainstorming for the prompt "Tell me about your family."

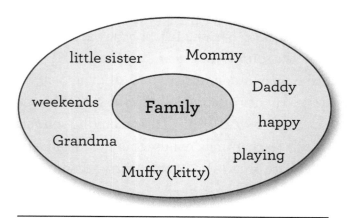

Figure 2.1: Prewriting showing brainstorming.

Next, the teacher models transferring key information from the brainstormed list to a graphic organizer that illustrates the sequence of the story (such as in figure 2.2). Depending on the genre and the grade, each portion of the map may represent an idea, a sentence, or a paragraph.

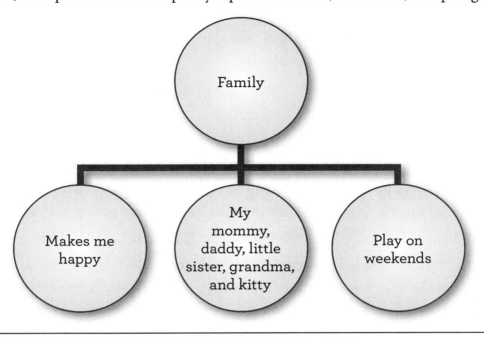

Figure 2.2: Prewriting graphic organizer showing sequencing of ideas.

The teacher should model the writing of an opening sentence or paragraph that addresses who, what, and when questions; students then mirror crafting an opening. Teachers can also add additional details beneath each portion of the sequence map, such as introductions and conclusions, problems and resolutions, and various other organizational features. The students then mirror this step.

Next, the teacher models a closing that avoids trite sentiments. As students demonstrate readiness and as grade-level standards dictate, the teacher should model adding transition words, with students mirroring this important step.

The teacher should then reinforce the notion that we can say (or draw) what we think and write what we say. He or she can do so by modeling oral rehearsal, or "talking" the first draft based on the notes organized in the map. Students should then do the same, perhaps in pairs, after having been taught to listen and provide constructive feedback. In fact, students should have opportunities to orally rehearse with many different partners as they create their first draft. Finally, the teacher might conference with students, particularly those who would benefit from additional support.

This may seem like a great deal of prewriting—perhaps more than most teachers have ever done. This is entirely intentional. The goal is to help students craft their best first draft. Revising and editing are difficult tasks, and students may not always be highly committed and motivated. While they must complete the absolutely essential steps of revising and editing, the more time they spend prewriting, the higher the quality of their finished products. The goal in modeling and extensively prewriting is to equip students with skills so they can write more independently. As the school year progresses, and as school years progress, teachers gradually release responsibility to students. While teachers still guide the writing process, they include less modeling and mirroring.

Drafting

After prewriting but before drafting, teachers may decide to begin the entire writing process with a new prompt but fewer teacher scaffolds, or they may ask students to save the prewriting for future use, or they may continue the writing process with the same piece through the next steps of the process, all the way to publishing. The point is that not every prompt-driven, rubric-guided writing endeavor needs be taken all the way through the process to publishing.

Now that teachers have devoted purposeful and productive time to organizing and planning for prewriting, it's time to write a well-developed, best first draft. This starts with the teacher thinking aloud to model how sentences and paragraphs are constructed based on the map. Students should then mirror the teacher's model based on their own maps, either independently or with partners. For example, a best first draft based on the previous prewriting example may appear as follows:

> My family is important to me. My family makes me happy because they are always kind to me. My family and I all live together in our apartment. The members of my family are my mommy, daddy, little sister, grandma, and kitty. I take care of my little sister and kitty, and my grandma takes care of me. My favorite thing about my family is that we play a lot on weekends. I love my family very much.

Revising

Based on the teacher and students' analysis of an anchor paper and guided by the rubric for this particular piece of writing, students then begin the process of improving their draft with information from the teacher and student feedback given via a rubric. Examples appear later in the chapter along with a more detailed description. The teacher should model this process, thinking aloud how his or her modeled piece of writing compares to the anchor paper and the rubric. Students should independently and with partners mirror this feedback. Based on the focus for the current piece of writing (such as transitions) and the teacher's assessment of student needs, the teacher then provides mini-lessons to help students successfully revise their drafts, either individually or in small-group teacher-student conferences.

Editing

During the editing phase of the writing process, the teacher should model how to correct grammatical and mechanical errors in the modeled piece of writing. Focus should be on editing skills that have previously been taught, as well as on any focus that the teacher has chosen for this particular piece of writing. Mini-lessons may again be appropriate. Teachers should also use oral rehearsal during the revising and editing components of the writing process so that students can hear what their writing sounds like and so their peers can practice analyzing the work of others.

Publishing

The teacher should model composing a final draft based on the revisions and edits, along with how to craft a published version using legible printing, cursive writing, or word processing. Students then mirror the teacher's model with their own piece of writing. Publishing should conclude by giving students time to share their writing through author's chair or in small groups. Students occupying the author's chair can share with the whole class or a small group.

Finally, students should reflect on their work, with special attention paid to how their writing has grown and improved.

Following an Instructional Sequence

The instructional sequence of a writing process may follow the following cycle:

- **Week 1**—Model prewriting, drafting, revising, and editing for a given prompt in the genre, with students sharing in a classroom writing effort.

- **Week 2**—Guide students through prewriting, drafting, revising, and editing for a new prompt in the genre, gradually releasing responsibility to students from whole-class writing, to pair writing, to individual writing.

- **Week 3**—Release students who have demonstrated the readiness to prewrite, draft, revise, edit, and publish with structured independence, while providing more small-group, guided support to students who have not yet demonstrated a readiness to work independently.

Systematically and explicitly modeling writing and then gradually releasing responsibility to students is necessary if educators truly expect all students to produce high-quality writing. Visit **go.solution-tree.com/rti** to view a proposed writing scope and sequence for a year in each grade level from kindergarten to third grade.

Making Time for Writing

In addition to the more structured and guided writing instruction described in the previous section, students should also have daily time to draw and write on topics and in styles of their choosing. Writing is a form of self-expression and a critical way in which students will be asked to express themselves throughout their lives. Consider the following strategies:

- Open or close instructional blocks with free-writes or loosely defined prompts to which students respond in a journal that they maintain throughout the year. Journal entries need not be assessed; they can be checked for completion, or they can serve as a point of conversation during writing conferences.

- Ask students to use their free-writing journals to practice writing with a certain voice and style, or for a particular purpose and audience, while also practicing the conventions and grammar they have recently learned.

- During independent practice, direct students to spend time adding to their free-writing journals.

Structured and free writing should both be part of writing every day, and writing should be part of reading, mathematics, and all other content areas. Teachers can look for general, loosely defined prompt ideas, such as on the Can Teach K–3 Learning Pages (www.canteach.ca/elementary /prompts.html).

Writing Assessment

In the spirit of universal screening and early intervention, teachers should administer a snapshot of writing (SOW) to students—a brief, on-demand prompt that asks students to write on a topic that is not dependent on prior knowledge or content knowledge. Teachers should give the SOW at the beginning of the school year to quickly identify students significantly at risk in the area of writing. Since many kindergarten students have not yet received instruction in writing, the SOW in kindergarten may be more helpful in revealing students with accelerated readiness levels. Teachers need not assess the SOW exhaustively in the same manner as process and published writing that uses analytic rubrics. Rather, assessments of SOWs should be quick: is the student desperately at risk in writing, which will impact success in all content areas and could indicate other difficulties? The purpose of a SOW is efficient early identification of students who may be at high risk for experiencing difficulties in the area of written expression. If teachers can identify students for whom writing is a major difficulty, they can both intervene and scaffold instruction. Possible SOW prompts include:

- **Kindergarten**—Draw and write a story about your family.
- **First grade**—Write a story about your favorite moment from kindergarten.
- **Second grade**—Write a story about your favorite moment from this past summer.
- **Third grade**—Write a story about your best friend.

Instead of an analytic rubric, use a simplified rubric (such as those shown in tables 2.3 through 2.6 on pages 63–64) to assess SOWs. These samples include descriptors from the Common Core.

Table 2.3: Kindergarten SOW Rubric

Ideas	Organization	Voice, Word Choice, and Fluency	Conventions
Drawing includes: - Discernible characters - Discernible settings - Appropriate colors, parts, and characteristics	- Spacing between words and sentences exists. - Writing moves from left to right and top to bottom.	- Student reading of drawing or writing makes sense. - Writing follows a sequence that can be logically followed by the reader.	- Letters and words are spaced correctly. - Letters can typically be identified. - There are attempts to use capitalization and punctuation.

Table 2.4: First-Grade SOW Rubric

Ideas	Organization	Voice, Word Choice, and Fluency	Conventions
- Focus is generally maintained on a single topic. - All parts of the prompt are fully addressed. - Ideas are communicated in three or more related sentences.	- Story tells who and where. - Spacing between words and sentences is appropriate. - Writing moves from left to right and top to bottom.	- Simple subjects and predicates are discernible in writing.	- Simple words are spelled correctly. - Spelling of more difficult words is phonetic and does not interfere with understanding. - Writing is legible and neat. - Sentences have correct capitalization and punctuation.

Table 2.5: Second-Grade SOW Rubric

Ideas	Organization	Voice, Word Choice, and Fluency	Conventions
The writing: • Addresses the prompt • Begins with a topic sentence • Relates to the prompt (all sentences) • Has an ending that wraps up the story	• Story tells who, what, where, and when. • Key words and questions from the prompt are addressed. • Spacing between words and sentences is appropriate.	• Adjectives and adverbs modify nouns and verbs. • Verbs are varied. • Each sentence is complete. • Simple transition words move the story along.	• The writing has few mechanical errors that interfere with readability. • The writing is legible. • Verbs typically match subjects.

Table 2.6: Third-Grade SOW Rubric

Ideas	Organization	Voice, Word Choice, and Fluency	Conventions
The writing: • Addresses the prompt • Maintains a focus • Starts with a beginning that grabs the reader's attention • Has an ending that wraps up the story	• Opening paragraph tells who, what, where, and when. • Story includes a notable beginning, middle, and end. • Related sentences are grouped into paragraphs.	• Some verbs are active. • Each sentence is complete. • Sentences flow logically. • Transition words help move the story along.	• The writing has few mechanical errors that interfere with readability. • The writing is legible. • Verbs typically match subjects. • The writing includes some complete compound sentences.

Using Analytic Rubrics to Guide Writing

Analytic rubrics are the ultimate formative assessments. When well designed and well used, they can focus current instruction and help determine future instruction. Remember, when guiding and assessing writing, particularly when using rubrics that are rich with details, consider focusing on portions of the rubric, perhaps based on the needs of students. For example, based on an assessment of student needs or based on current areas of curricular focus, the teacher may choose to focus on fluency (such as how transition words help move the story along) or an area of conventions (such as comparative and superlative adjectives and how they are used appropriately). Also, when using any rubric, teachers should collaborate with their peers to build greater inter-rater reliability—simply read samples of student writing from a variety of classrooms. Not only will colleagues determine if their definition of *proficiency* is aligned, but teachers will learn about student needs and perhaps also about the instructional strengths of other teachers. Tables 2.7 through 2.10 (pages 66–69) show suggested analytic rubrics based on the six traits of writing. Unlike SOW rubrics, these rubrics are used to more deeply analyze the strengths and areas for improvement in student writing.

Analytic rubrics should be designed so that feedback to students is clear, specific, and efficiently given. Teachers can highlight elements of the rubric on which students should focus during the revising and editing process, as well as identify students' relative areas of strength.

Writing Interventions

As in all content areas, writing intervention requires additional time and targeted support. It involves meeting the students where they are, determining where in the developmental process of writing their skills lie, and building their skills toward grade-level proficiency. Difficulties with written expression may also be evident through difficulties with oral expression. Information gained from SOWs and other writing assignments is critical in the day-to-day core instructional experiences of the student in the classroom and for determination of necessary supports.

When a measure such as the SOW indicates that a student may experience serious challenges in writing, schools and teachers must identify alternative ways that the student can demonstrate understanding. If writing is an area of difficulty, perhaps students can express mastery orally, through graphic organizers that do not require as much writing, or through drawings. Additionally, students can produce written responses, but with more support and scaffolds, such as sentence frames that require students to insert key words.

Teachers give SOWs to identify students at risk in the area of writing so that they can be proactive and intervene early in the school year. These proactive supports take two forms. First, they provide supplemental supports at a student's current level, with the expectation that he or she will work toward closing the gap between his or her current level and grade-level proficiency. Second, teachers scaffold and modify the written language requirements within the classroom so that a student's difficulty in writing does not compromise his or her ability to demonstrate mastery of mathematics, social studies, science, and so on.

Table 2.7: Kindergarten Analytic Rubric

Ideas	Organization	Voice, Word Choice, and Fluency	Conventions

• Drawing and writing:
  + Include discernible characters
  + Include discernible settings
  + Include appropriate colors, parts, characteristics, and functionality (in pictures)
  + Generally maintain focus on a single topic
• All parts of writing task are fully addressed.
• Ideas are communicated independently in three or more related sentences.
	• Story tells who and where.
	• Sentence(s) relate to the prompt.
	• Spacing between words and sentences is appropriate.
	• Writing moves from left to right and top to bottom.
		• Story begins to have a purpose.
		• Story begins to address an audience.
		• Writing matches the picture.
		• Simple subjects and predicates are discernible in writing.
		• Student "reading" of writing makes sense.
		• Writing follows a sequence that can be logically followed by the reader.
		• Student's voice is evident.
			• Student attempts to phonetically spell more difficult words that do not interfere with the reader's understanding.
			• Letters and words are spaced correctly.
			• Writing is legible and neat.
			• Sentences have correct capitalization and ending punctuation.
			• The following are used appropriately:
			  + Printing
			  + Nouns
			  + Verbs
			  + Regular plural nouns
			  + Question words
			  + Prepositions
			  + Capitalization
			  + Punctuation
			  + Phonetic spelling

Table 2.8: First-Grade Analytic Rubric

Ideas	Organization	Voice, Word Choice, and Fluency	Conventions
The writing: • Addresses the prompt (directly or indirectly) • Opens with a lead topic sentence • Has minimal unrelated information • Maintains focus • Tells a story of one experience • Has an ending that wraps up the story	• Story tells who, what, where, and when. • Key words and questions from the prompt are addressed in the story. • Closing sentence expresses a thought, reaction, feeling, or opinion. • Story includes a purposeful and notable beginning and end. • Story identifies a problem and a resolution. • The beginning tells what the narrative is about.	• Sentence pattern shows some variation. • Story begins to address an audience or reader. • Story begins to have a purpose. • Adjectives and adverbs appropriately modify nouns and verbs. • Verbs are varied. • Selected words are specific, not general. • Each sentence is complete. • Sentences generally flow in a logical fashion. • The events are in order and the writing includes time words and phrases. • Simple transition words move the story along. • Use of quotation marks is not excessive. • The writing sounds like someone is talking. • The writing shows evidence of the students own voice or style.	• Includes complete and coherent sentences. • Includes few mechanical errors that interfere with readability. • Letters, words, and sentences are spaced appropriately. • The writing is legible. • The following (and conventions from kindergarten) are used appropriately: + Letter formation + Common nouns + Proper nouns + Possessive nouns + Possessive pronouns + Indefinite pronouns + Past-tense verbs + Present-tense verbs + Future-tense verbs + Adjectives + Conjunctions + Determiners + Simple sentences + Compound sentences + Subject-verb agreement + Personal pronouns + Capitalization + Punctuation + Spelling

Table 2.9: Second-Grade Analytic Rubric

Ideas	Organization	Voice, Word Choice, and Fluency	Conventions
The writing: • Addresses the prompt • Opens with a lead or topic sentence in the beginning and in each paragraph • Directly or indirectly addresses the prompt (every sentence) • Does not include unrelated information • Maintains focus • Tells a true story of one experience • Starts with a beginning that grabs the reader's attention • Uses details to help the reader imagine the experience • Has an ending that wraps up the story	• Opening paragraph tells who, what, where, and when. • In narrative writing, the opening paragraph introduces characters and settings. • Key words and questions from the prompt are addressed in the opening sentence (or paragraph). • Closing sentence (or paragraph) expresses a thought, reaction, feeling, or opinion. • Story includes a purposeful and notable beginning, middle, and end. • Story identifies a problem and a resolution. • The writing has related sentences grouped into paragraphs.	• Sentence pattern is varied. • Story begins to address an audience or reader. • Story begins to have a purpose. • Adjectives and adverbs are rich. • Verbs are active. • Words begin to allow the reader to visualize the events, characters, or objects described. • Each sentence is complete. • Sentences flow logically. • Transition words help move the story along. • The writer tells the events in order using time words and phrases. • Detail sentences directly follow main idea sentences. • Use of quotation marks is not excessive. • Writing shows evidence of student's own voice and style. • Writing holds reader's attention. • Writing reads like someone is talking.	• The writing has complete and coherent sentences. • Errors do not interfere with understanding. • The writing is legible. • The following (and conventions from K–1) are used appropriately: 　+ Nouns 　+ Irregular plural nouns 　+ Reflexive pronouns 　+ Past tense of irregular verbs 　+ Adjectives 　+ Adverbs 　+ Complete simple sentences 　+ Complete compound sentences 　+ Capitalization 　+ Commas 　+ Possessives 　+ Spelling

Table 2.10: Third-Grade Analytic Rubric

Ideas	Organization	Voice, Word Choice, and Fluency	Conventions

The writing:
• Addresses the prompt (all sentences)
• Maintains focus
• Has a main idea in each paragraph
• Has at least three specific details with each main idea
• Tells of one experience
• Grabs the reader's attention at the beginning
• Uses details to create context for the reader to imagine the experience
• Includes only important events and details
	• Opening paragraph tells who, what, where, and when.
	• In narrative writing, the opening paragraph introduces characters and settings.
	• Key words and questions from the prompt are addressed in the opening paragraph.
	• Closing paragraph expresses a thought, reaction, feeling, or opinion.
	• Story includes a purposeful and notable beginning, middle, and end, with a significantly longer middle.
		• Similes are incorporated.
		• Metaphors are used.
		• Words or short phrases vary the rhythm of sentences.
		• Story addresses an audience or reader.
		• Story has a purpose.
		• Adjectives and adverbs are rich and varied.
		• Verbs are specific and strong.
		• Words allow the reader to visualize the events, characters, or objects described.
		• Each sentence is complete.
		• Sentences flow logically and sequentially.
		• Subtle transition words symbolize passage of time or sequence of events.
		• Events are told in order using time words and phrases.
			• The writing includes complete and coherent sentences.
			• The writing includes a variety of sentence types.
			• Errors do not interfere with understanding.
			• The writing has correct margins and spacing.
			• The writing is legible.
			• The following (and conventions from K–2) are used appropriately:
			  + Nouns
			  + Pronouns
			  + Verbs
			  + Adjectives
			  + Adverbs
			  + Regular plural nouns
			  + Irregular plural nouns
			  + Abstract nouns
			  + Regular sentences
			  + Irregular sentences
			  + Simple verb tenses
			  + Subject-verb agreement

continued ↓

Ideas	Organization	Voice, Word Choice, and Fluency	Conventions

The writing:
 	
• Details why the experience was memorable
 	
• Has an ending that wraps up the story
	• Story identifies a problem and a resolution.
	
	• Paragraphs signal the introduction of new ideas.
		• Writing shows evidence of author's voice and style.
		
		• Writing holds reader's attention, using dialogue as appropriate.
		
		• Word choice is accurate and clear.
			• The following (and conventions from K–2) are used appropriately:
			
			  + Pronoun-antecedent agreement
			
			  + Comparative and superlative adjectives
			
			  + Comparative and superlative adverbs
			
			  + Coordinating conjunctions
			
			  + Subordinating conjunctions
			
			  + Simple sentences
			
			  + Compound sentences
			
			  + Complex sentences
			
			  + Capitalization
			
			  + Commas
			
			  + Possessives
			
			  + Spelling

Results from SOWs, combined with other, ongoing formal and informal assessments of student writing, will reveal students with differentiated writing needs. The developmental, product-oriented nature of writing should help clarify the specific supports students need. Students at risk in writing may be well served with intervention focused on earlier grade-level standards, as they typically represent skill prerequisites that students may not have mastered. Similarly, students who demonstrate high levels of proficiency relative to the current grade-level standards may be ready for extension and enrichment as outlined by the writing expectations of the next grade level.

For example, a first-grade student who demonstrates a high level of readiness may proceed beyond the first-grade standards of opening with a purposeful lead topic sentence, using adjectives and adverbs that appropriately modify nouns and verbs, and incorporating varied verbs and simple transition words to move the story along. The teacher may extend student learning to greater depths and levels of complexity, as represented by second-grade standards, such as opening with a purposeful lead sentence that grabs the reader's attention and tells who, what, where, and when; using rich adjectives and adverbs that help the reader imagine the story; and incorporating active verbs that allow the reader to visualize events.

Similarly, a first-grade student with lower levels of readiness may receive scaffolds and targeted instruction that help the student rapidly reach grade-level expectations. This student may temporarily benefit from supports typically associated with kindergarten.

As Richard Allington (2009) has written about reading:

> The single-most critical factor that will determine the success of the effort is matching struggling readers with texts they can actually read with a high level of accuracy, fluency, and comprehension. (p. 45)

The same applies to writing. For students with levels of readiness that place them at risk of not reaching grade-level expectations, teachers must intervene, provide supplemental supports, and most importantly, have higher expectations for the rates of growth these students will demonstrate. The intent is to provide these supports only temporarily. We must expect the student to respond to these interventions and to make progress that will eliminate the need for scaffolds so that he or she produces writing at grade level.

More Structured Supports for At-Risk Writers

In addition to targeting writing instruction at the student's current readiness level, there are two other practical steps that can assist students with more intensive writing needs. First, teachers can explore the writing-reading connection. Students who have difficulty with reading skills (such as phonics and comprehension) may have difficulty with writing (such as encoding and expressing comprehensible thoughts in written form). If students are having difficulties writing, consider that they may be experiencing challenges in reading as well, and diagnose and address the challenges immediately. Kate Kinsella (2005) summarizes this reading-writing connection:

- Reading from a variety of genres and reading frequently leads to better writing.

- Reading aloud often to children, particularly when they are young, contributes to students becoming good writers.

- To improve writing, increase the frequency with which students read and write.

- Emerging writers must be exposed to and must collectively analyze multiple models.

The second practical step is to further help students structure and organize their thoughts and writing using key symbols or colors (see *Step up to Writing* [Auman, 2003]). Teachers can apply color coding to prewriting or drafts. Green corresponds with beginning sentences and paragraphs that express the main topic of the piece of writing. Yellow corresponds with reasons, details, or facts that are related to the main topic. Red corresponds with examples that support the reasons, details, or facts. (The color red reminds students to stop and add support before continuing with the piece.) Green can be used again, this time to conclude the writing (by signaling to the student to look back to the beginning sentence or paragraph to cohesively conclude).

This type of intervention may seem formulaic. It uses a highly structured form of writing, but it's temporary. The goal is for students to develop a love of writing and to revise and edit their work; however, when students cannot produce written words on a page, they will neither develop a love of writing nor create a piece of writing that can be revised and edited.

Preventative Supports for All Students

The following supports will help prevent writing difficulties for students and provide the structures necessary for teachers to intervene early:

- Prominently display students' written work in the classroom.

- Make time for students to write daily, both in a free-response journal and as part of the writing process.

- Provide a risk-free writing environment that is focused on growth and improvement.

- Ensure that peer-to-peer and student-teacher conferences occur daily.

- Model thinking and actions throughout the writing process, and give students the opportunity to immediately mirror this modeling.

- Set a predictable writing routine during which students are encouraged to think, reflect, and revise.

- Allow students to publish and share their work, followed by time for reflection and further rewriting.

- Make the reading-writing connection explicit.

- Make writing a part of every content area.

The Four Questions of RTI in Writing

Teacher teams and schoolwide teams should regularly consider the following four questions when determining whether students are responding to instruction and intervention (Buffum et al., 2012):

1. **About which students do we have concerns?** Schools should screen for writing, perhaps using the snapshot of writing (SOW) to efficiently determine who may need additional support early in the school year. Because writing is a daily part of instruction, students with other writing needs should be identified throughout the year.

2. **In what areas do we have concerns?** Analytic rubrics allow for the diagnosis of writing needs. Remember that writing needs may be linked to difficulties in reading.

3. **What are we currently doing to support the student and meet the student's needs?** The scaffolds and developmentally appropriate supports described in this chapter can help target instruction and intervention at the student's current levels of readiness.

4. **Has the student responded to the instruction and interventions (the supports) that we have been providing?** Teams should track writing by maintaining a portfolio of dated student samples, both those formally and informally assessed, both with and without analytic rubrics.

Summary

For some students, a blank page is not a challenge—it's a curse. These students face obstacles with ideas, organization, and writing structures that prevent them from producing writing. Writing is absolutely critical; it is the only curricular area identified as an element of 90/90/90 schools (Reeves, 2000). Educators must ensure that all students can successfully communicate their thoughts and understandings in writing. Schools must provide students with supportive environments in which they revise, edit, and publish. To help students, teachers must explicitly model the writing process, gradually releasing responsibility to students to write more authentically and independently. Use the reproducible Guiding Goals for K–3 Writing checklist (page 74) to help determine the next steps you will take (in your classroom, team, school, or district) in your RTI-based writing program.

The next chapter focuses on research, content, instruction, assessment, and intervention in mathematics. Mathematics is intricately linked to reading and writing. Like reading and writing, there are multiple schools of thought concerning how students best learn mathematics. By examining the most current research in mathematics and combining the best practices from various approaches, educators can ensure that every student leaves third grade ready to attack the more complex mathematics of fourth grade and beyond.

Guiding Goals for K–3 Writing

Goal	Long-Term Vision	First Steps
Fully understand all approaches to teaching writing and learning to write, and collaboratively develop a horizontally and vertically articulated plan	Staff blend the strategies and routines from the best practices in writing to ensure that all students write well and effectively communicate their thinking.	☐ All staff engage in collaborative study of the best practices in writing, including but not limited to writers' workshop, process writing, 6 + 1 traits, *Write From the Beginning*, and *Step up to Writing*. ☐ All staff eagerly and actively participate in professional development in writing. ☐ Staff begin to employ and refine effective writing practices that address the prewriting, drafting, revising, editing, and publishing needs of all students.
Develop and utilize rubrics to inform teaching and learning in writing	Staff employ rubrics to drive instruction so that all students write increasingly well.	☐ Staff collaboratively develop rubrics. ☐ Through collegial readings of student writing from across the school, teachers improve inter-rater reliability and determine the most immediate student learning needs.
Administer universal screeners, and support identified students in need	Staff administer writing screeners three times a year and support students in need in the area of writing through supplemental intervention and in-class scaffolds.	☐ Staff administer and efficiently assess brief writing probes to determine students at grave risk in writing. ☐ The school builds a system of support for students who require intensive supports in improving their written expression. ☐ Staff explore and employ effective strategies within the classroom so that students can demonstrate their mastery of content in alternative ways.

RTI in the Early Grades © 2013 Solution Tree Press • solution-tree.com
Visit **go.solution-tree.com/rti** to download this page.

| Scope and sequence writing genres and blend instruction in written conventions into the authentic teaching and learning of writing | Staff collaboratively design units of instruction in writing that explicitly teach students to write across multiple genres and employ mini-lessons to build the written convention skills of all students. | ☐ Staff devote significant time to student writing daily.

☐ Staff analyze state standards or CCSS in writing and sequence instruction in writing and writing genres.

☐ Staff unpack skills associated with written conventions (such as grammar, mechanics, and spelling), provide explicit instruction in these areas, and employ mini-lessons to improve student use of conventions within authentic writing. |
| Teach students to write | Teacher teams collaboratively develop and employ instructional practices that model effective writing through prewriting, drafting, revising, editing, and publishing, followed by multiple opportunities for students to first mirror teacher models and then independently write. | ☐ Teacher teams explore and craft instructional practices in writing.

☐ Teachers use rubrics and anchor papers to set a target for writing.

☐ Teachers explicitly model effective writing habits and the writing process.

☐ Teachers facilitate and guide multiple opportunities for students to model teacher writing.

☐ Teachers facilitate and guide multiple opportunities for students to write independently. |

RTI in the Early Grades © 2013 Solution Tree Press • solution-tree.com
Visit **go.solution-tree.com/rti** to download this page.

CHAPTER 3

Mathematics

Many who have had an opportunity of knowing . . . about mathematics confuse it with arithmetic, and consider it an arid science. In reality, however, it is a science which requires a great amount of imagination.

SOFIA KOVALEVSKAYA

Success in mathematics may have a direct bearing on an individual's and a nation's economic well-being. Research suggests that a student's performance in mathematics better predicts his or her future earnings and other economic outcomes than other skills learned in high school (American Diploma Project, 2004). Early success in number sense is the best predictor of later success in mathematics and reading, and the converse is true; difficulties in kindergarten and first grade in number sense predict later difficulties in mathematics and reading (Duncan et al., 2007). Indeed, the percentage of students in the class of 2009 who were highly accomplished in math is well below that of most countries with which the United States generally compares itself (Hanushek, Peterson, & Woessmann, 2011). A majority of nations participating in the Programme for International Student Assessment (PISA) mathematics test had a larger percentage of students than the United States who scored at the advanced level, and even the highest performing U.S. students did not score that well when compared internationally. Even when international comparisons only include students from families of affluence, the percentage of U.S. students performing at the highest levels is low compared to most countries (Organisation for Economic Co-operation and Development [OECD], 2011).

Countries with students who perform at higher levels in math and science show an increase in economic productivity over otherwise similar countries with lower performing students (Hanushek, Jamison, Jamison, & Woessmann, 2008). If educators believe that students' performance in mathematics is important to their future and to the nation's success, then it's time to consider a change: we must identify students who lack number sense immediately in kindergarten and provide instruction and intervention in the early grades.

Research on Early Mathematics

From 2000 to 2003 there were historic increases in the percentage of students scoring proficient on NAEP in fourth grade (from 65 percent to 77 percent); however, since then, the performance of fourth graders has been stagnant. A similar pattern exists in eighth grade, although the change from 2000 to 2003 was much less positive. From 1978 to 2004, the overall mathematics performance of seventeen-year-old students in the United States changed only slightly (Kloosterman, 2010). We should perhaps not be surprised that nearly one in three students fails algebra (Higgins, 2008).

Looking at international trends sheds further light on U.S. students' mathematics achievement. Only 6 percent of students in the United States scored at the advanced level on the 2009 PISA examinations, compared to 28 percent of students in Taiwan and significantly higher percentages in Hong Kong, Korea, and Finland. In fact, sixteen countries had more than twice the percentage of advanced students as the United States, and students from another fourteen countries outperformed U.S. students. Only four countries underperformed U.S. students: Portugal, Greece, Turkey, and Mexico (OECD, 2011).

The Trends in International Mathematics and Science Study (TIMSS) compares the mathematics and science skills of fourth- and eighth-grade students and includes more underdeveloped nations than the PISA testing. In 2007, the average mathematics scores of students in the United States were higher than the overall TIMSS average. The average U.S. fourth-grade mathematics score was higher than those of students in twenty-three of the thirty-five other countries and lower than those in eight countries, all located in Asia or Europe. The average U.S. eighth-grade mathematics score was higher than those of students in thirty-seven of the forty-seven other countries and lower than those in five countries, all located in Asia. In 2007, 10 percent of U.S. fourth graders and 6 percent of U.S. eighth graders scored at or above the advanced international benchmark in mathematics. In fourth grade, seven countries had higher percentages of students performing at or above the advanced international mathematics benchmark. In eighth grade as well, seven countries had higher percentages of students performing at or above the advanced mathematics benchmark. While the TIMSS scores of U.S. students have increased since 1995, the growth of U.S. students has been in the middle of the pack (Gonzales et al., 2008).

These international comparisons of the performance of U.S. students in mathematics are concerning. Clearly we must reconsider how we are teaching mathematics and what is being taught, and this extends into the early grades.

A Blended Approach to Early Mathematics

Part of the mathematics debate is the efficacy of algorithmic (procedural or step-by-step) approaches for deductively solving math problems versus more inquiry-based, constructivist (conceptual) approaches for inductively solving math problems (Rittle-Johnson, Siegler, & Alibali, 2001).

While research favors the former approach, the limited efficacy of more inquiry-based approaches seems to stem from a lack of readiness on the part of students and teachers—not because the approach itself is not sound. Mathematics policy groups have recommended a middle ground (Hiebert, 1999).

As is the case in reading and writing, the best approach is to embrace the "Genius of And" and avoid the polarization that results from the "Tyranny of Or" (Collins, 2001). For example, the development of automaticity and fluency are compatible with computation and problem-solving abilities and should be equally valued. Conceptual and procedural awareness are both valuable and reinforce one another (Rittle-Johnson et al., 2001; Wurman & Wilson, 2012). The critical point is to focus curriculum and to engage in more depth and less breadth of study.

The National Council of Teachers of Mathematics (NCTM) developed its *Focal Points* for kindergarten through eighth grade (Schielack et al., 2006) to counteract the tendency within curricula to ask students to master a wide range of topics in a short period of time, preventing them from developing a depth of understanding. The NCTM recommendations for kindergarten through third grade are summarized in table 3.1. They have several implications. The focus on number sense is noteworthy, and the emphasis on depth over breadth is significant.

Table 3.1: Summary of NCTM Focal Points

Skills	Kindergarten	First Grade	Second Grade	Third Grade
Numbers and operations and algebra	Represent, compare, and order whole numbers, and join them to and remove them from sets.	Understand whole number relationships, addition and subtraction, strategies for basic addition and related subtraction facts.	Understand base-ten numbers, place value, and multidigit addition and subtraction.	Understand fractions, multiplication, and division.
Geometry	Describe shapes and space.	Compose and decompose geometric shapes.		Describe and analyze properties of two-dimensional shapes.
Measurement	Order objects by measurable attributes.		Understand linear measurement, and develop facility in measuring lengths.	

Source: Schielack et al., 2006.

In 2008, the National Mathematics Advisory Panel (NMAP) released its final report, based on an analysis of years of research by leading national mathematics experts. The panel released forty-five recommendations, which are summarized as follows:

- Elementary and middle school mathematics content should be focused, without spiral review of content from year to year.

- K–8 mathematics should focus on fractions, decimals, and percents. Proficiency with whole numbers is a prerequisite for the study of fractions, decimals, percents, measurement, and geometry, and is the critical foundation of algebra.

- Schools should prepare more students to take algebra by grade 8.

- Most children acquire knowledge of numbers before entering kindergarten. Children from low-income backgrounds enter school with far less knowledge than their peers from middle-income backgrounds, and the achievement gap progressively widens.

- Strategies exist that have been shown to improve the mathematical knowledge of kindergarteners, especially those from low-income backgrounds.

- To prepare students for algebra, curriculum must simultaneously develop conceptual understanding, computational fluency, and problem-solving skills. Debates regarding the relative importance of these aspects of mathematical knowledge are misguided. These areas are mutually supportive.

- Computational proficiency with whole numbers depends on sufficient practice to develop automaticity, using the commutative, distributive, and associative properties.

- A conceptual understanding of fractions and decimals and the operational procedures for using them are mutually reinforcing. Students should be able to represent fractions on a number line.

- Students' goals and beliefs about learning are related to their performance. Changing children's beliefs from a focus on ability to a focus on effort increases their engagement.

- Educators assume that students need to be a certain age to learn certain mathematical ideas. However, developmental appropriateness is largely contingent on prior opportunities to learn. Claims that children cannot learn certain content because they are too young or not developmentally ready have consistently been shown to be wrong.

- U.S. mathematics textbooks are too long, and this length contributes to a lack of coherence. Mathematics textbooks are much smaller in nations with higher mathematics achievement than the United States. One contributor to the length of books is the demand to meet varying state standards.

- Publishers must ensure the mathematical accuracy of their materials.

The lessons from the NMAP provide both pragmatic suggestions and a call to action—if we are to succeed in changing and improving the mathematics performance of students, we are going to have to do things differently.

Perhaps the NMAP's most immediate and important recommendation is to make the mathematical areas of focus from kindergarten through eighth grade more streamlined, well-defined, and well-understood. Educators should avoid approaches that revisit topics year after year or several times within a year. Moreover, depth of knowledge and proficiency with whole numbers and fractions (and their equivalent representations—decimals and percents) are the critical foundations of algebra. In addition, educators must embrace, understand, and explicitly teach in a way that recognizes that conceptual and procedural understandings are equally important and mutually reinforcing. Also, students must have an active involvement in their mathematics learning, and teachers should realize that most students develop considerable knowledge of mathematics before kindergarten. These recommendations should drive our revisions to math instruction in the early grades. We must concentrate our instruction. We are attempting to cover too much material; students who do not respond to initial math instruction may simply be drowning under an excessive number of standards in a given grade level. Obtaining mastery and depth of knowledge of a more concise set of standards will accomplish much, including fewer casualties of a mile-wide, inch-deep core math curriculum. The most important tier in RTI is Tier 1, the core curriculum that every student should receive. The instructional and differentiated practices within Tier 1 represent the fundamentals and foundations of RTI.

Key Mathematics Content

Reports from PISA (OECD, 2011) and TIMSS (Gonzales et al., 2008), the Final Report of the NMAP (2008), and the National Council of Teachers of Mathematics (Schielack et al., 2006) led to the development of the CCSS in 2008. Table 3.2 (page 82) provides a broad overview of the CCSS in mathematics.

The CCSS have the potential to refine our work, specifically in the area of focusing content (more depth, less breadth) and emphasizing instructional practices. Critical consumers of the CCSS in mathematics will notice that they are not as rigorous, focused, or clear as some state standards and most standards from high-performing nations, but they are more rigorous, focused, and clear than many state standards (Wurman & Wilson, 2012). They emphasize the importance of making explicit and frequent connections to previously learned content and to the applications of multiplication and addition to non-number strands, such as area and volume. There is a notable focus on number sense in kindergarten through third grade (and on through fifth grade), depth is emphasized over breadth, and algebra content primarily begins in sixth grade. The similarity of standards in first and second grades may concern some educators; rigor should be emphasized in

Table 3.2: Summary of CCSS in Mathematics

Topic	Kindergarten	First Grade	Second Grade	Third Grade
Counting and cardinality	Know number names, count, and compare.			
Number and operations in base ten	Work with numbers 11–19 to gain foundations for place value.	Extend the counting sequence, understand place value, and use place value to help add and subtract.	Understand place value, and use place value to help add and subtract.	Use place value to perform multidigit arithmetic.
Operations and algebraic thinking	Understand addition as putting together and adding to, and subtraction as taking apart and taking from.	Represent and solve problems involving addition and subtraction within 20; understand the relationship between addition and subtraction (with simple equations).	Represent and solve problems involving addition and subtraction within 20, and work with equal groups to gain foundations for multiplication.	Represent and solve problems involving multiplication and division within 100, and understand the relationship between multiplication and division; solve problems involving the four operations, identifying and explaining patterns in arithmetic.
Number and operations—fractions				Develop understanding of fractions as numbers.
Measurement and data	Describe and compare measurable attributes, classify objects, and count the number of objects in categories.	Measure lengths indirectly and by iterating length units, telling time, and representing and interpreting data.	Measure and estimate lengths in standard units and relate to addition and subtraction; work with time and money, and represent and interpret data.	Solve problems involving measurement and the estimation of intervals of time, liquid volume, and mass; represent and interpret data; understand area and relate area to multiplication and addition; understand perimeter and distinguish between linear and area measures.
Geometry	Identify, describe, analyze, compare, create, and compose shapes.	Reason with shapes and their attributes.	Reason with shapes and their attributes.	Reason with shapes and their attributes.

Source: NGA & CCSSO, 2010b.

the primary grades. Some schools and school districts may find that their existing set of standards is actually more rigorous than the Common Core (Wurman & Wilson, 2012). Schools are wise to have vertical conversations between grade levels to ensure that spiraling of content from grade level to grade level is not inappropriate or does not detract from student mastery at greater levels of depth and complexity due to an excessive amount of focus on the prior grade level's content. While standards may appear to be the same, a more careful analysis will reveal differences in rigor.

The CCSS also emphasize eight mathematical practices:

1. Make sense of problems and persevere in problem solving.
2. Reason abstractly and quantitatively.
3. Construct and critique problem-solving arguments.
4. Model with mathematics.
5. Use appropriate tools.
6. Attend to precision.
7. Look for and make use of structure.
8. Look for and express regularity in repeated reasoning.

Students must be able to communicate their understanding verbally, in writing, and with models. These mathematical reasoning skills are vital to reinforcing depth over breadth in the scope and sequence of mathematics content. Given that a focused, standards-based (and a non-textbook-driven) approach to teaching mathematics will be relatively new for many teachers, school leaders should provide coherent professional development in these areas.

Key content starts with focused, articulated alignment. Working collaboratively, teachers should develop a scope and sequence that avoids excessive spiraling and does not necessarily follow the publisher's text, but instead focuses more depth and instructional days on the most essential standards. Teacher teams should unpack key content and standards and create common formative assessments, which is especially essential since the tests within publishers' texts may no longer match teacher-created pacing guides. Furthermore, teachers should be critical consumers of publishers' work. There are times when the rigor of the problems provided in textbooks relative to a given standard do not match the rigor required by the CCSS or state standards. The format of problems on which students will be asked to demonstrate mastery may also be mismatched.

The concept of number sense permeates all strands of mathematics and should be a focus throughout the year (Gersten, Clarke, Haymond, & Jordan, 2011; Wurman & Wilson, 2012). Number sense allows students to understand the meaning of numbers, decompose numbers, develop strategies for solving complex problems, make simple magnitude comparisons, create procedures for performing operations, and recognize appropriate estimates and inappropriate errors (Kalchman, Moss, &

Case, 2001). Number sense is critical to developing proficiency with mathematical procedures and understanding mathematical concepts. Number sense helps students develop a mental number line and also allows them to represent and manipulate quantities and solve a variety of mathematical problems.

Lack of number sense may contribute to learning difficulties and disabilities (Gersten & Chard, 1999). Explicit instruction in number sense reduces failure in early mathematics, and integrating number sense with computational fluency instruction benefits all students. In this way, number sense is analogous to phonemic awareness and phonics. Just as phonemic awareness and phonics are necessary for fluent reading and ultimately reading comprehension, number sense provides the foundation for other mathematics. Number sense instruction has the potential to help students build both computational fluency and problem-solving skills (Gersten & Chard, 1999).

Like language, number sense may be an inborn human skill (Dehaune, 1997), but many students require explicit, consistent supports to gain the depth of understanding necessary to apply number sense to higher mathematics. Students with mathematical disabilities may have a high frequency of procedural errors, difficulty in representing and retrieving facts, and an inability to symbolically or visually represent numerical information for storage (Gersten & Chard, 1999). These difficulties can be ameliorated through early, explicit instruction in number sense. Number sense is critical to conceptual understanding and to the application of procedural knowledge to new problems. Just as many students with early reading difficulties exhibit auditory problems, as evidenced through difficulties with phonological processing or phonemic awareness (Adams, 1990), many students with phonologically based reading difficulties have trouble with basic number sense; more than 60 percent of students with learning disabilities display significant difficulties in mathematics (Light & DeFries, 1995).

Mathematics has been an afterthought in the field of learning disabilities; problems with reading are the major source of referrals and diagnoses for learning disabilities (Light & DeFries, 1995). Math instruction too often focuses on mastery of algorithms with limited opportunities for students to explain their reasoning and receive feedback. Like early supports in phonological awareness, educators should focus attention on early and balanced instruction of number sense for students with learning disabilities or difficulties in mathematics. As a foundational skill for other mathematics concepts, number sense instruction should be explored both conceptually and procedurally in kindergarten, first, second, and third grade.

Mathematics Instruction

The eight mathematical practices emphasized in the CCSS, mentioned in the previous section on page 83, define the way in which students should demonstrate their understanding of mathematics and must therefore determine the ways in which mathematics is taught. Teachers should model how they reason through problems, how and why problem-solving steps and solutions are appropriate, and how to visually and narratively communicate solutions. Teachers often ask one question of students during the We Do It Together phase of instruction ("What is the correct answer?"), but they must increasingly ask a second and third question, questions that elicit responses to how and why mathematical problem-solving steps are appropriate. Procedural understanding is not sufficient; conceptual understanding involves asking how and why questions.

Focused content is critical, but pedagogy also matters a great deal. Research suggests seven key instructional practices for helping students learn mathematics (Jayanthi, Gersten, & Baker, 2008):

1. Teach students using explicit instruction on a regular basis.

2. Teach students using multiple instructional examples.

3. Have students verbalize decisions and solutions.

4. Teach students to visually represent information.

5. Teach students to solve problems using multiple strategies.

6. Provide ongoing formative assessment data and feedback to teachers.

7. Provide peer-assisted instruction to students.

Moreover, NMAP's recommendations (2008) extend beyond suggestions on the most appropriate scope and nature of content; the panel also made several pedagogical suggestions:

- Research does not support the exclusive use of either entirely student-centered or teacher-directed approaches.

- Cooperative, heterogeneous learning approaches have been shown to improve students' computation skills.

- Use of formative assessments improves student learning, especially when these assessments are used to individualize instruction.

- Explicit instruction (when teachers provide clear models for solving a problem, students extensively practice new strategies and skills, students are provided with opportunities to think aloud, and students are provided with extensive feedback) has resulted in consistently positive effects on solving word problems and computation.

These findings suggest that how we teach mathematics is at least as important as what we teach, a terrifically significant statement given that the sheer scope of standards is the greatest inhibitor to student success (Marzano et al., 2001). Instruction that gradually releases responsibility for learning to students; checks frequently for understanding and provides immediate, specific, corrective feedback; and employs simple and flexible engagement strategies is a must.

The same gradual-release model of instruction described in chapter 1 applies very successfully in mathematics (Jordan, Levine, & Huttenlocher, 1994; Kalchman et al., 2001). The direct instruction, gradual release of responsibility model has proven to be exceptionally successful in all teaching (Hattie, 2009) and specifically in teaching mathematics (Baker, Gersten, & Lee, 2002; Gersten et al., 2008). To review, following are the steps in that model:

1. Why Do It

2. I Do It

3. We Do It Together

4. You Do It Together

5. You Do It Alone

Teachers start by clearly communicating why that lesson (Why Do It) and the lesson's objective or learning target are critical and how they are connected to prior learning and the broader world. The teacher makes connections to the objective repeatedly throughout the lesson. He or she uses such strategies as tickets out the door or some other form of closure at the conclusion of the lesson to connect to and assess student mastery of the objective. To the extent possible, each lesson should address one focused learning target. At times, textbook lessons focus on multiple complex targets, which can result in a lack of success for students. They can cause teachers to rush lessons as they try to cover a large amount of content within a predetermined time, resulting in student confusion or a lack of depth of understating. Thus, when collaboratively planning mathematics instruction, teacher teams should ensure that a lesson's objective is focused.

During the I Do It phase, the teacher demonstratively models the solving of problems, with constant think-alouds and verbal, written, and graphic explanations that reveal why and how each step is taken. The teacher models how to use instructional strategies and steps, which are prominently posted in the classroom. Steps are a critical, temporary scaffold that are often absent from mathematics instruction. Well-designed steps help teachers explain the how and why behind mathematics thinking; they provide a task analysis of the problem-solving process. Steps can also help students practice their own problem solving in a step-by-step manner early in their development of proficiency so that they can later apply the skills to new situations. Finally, when used in a step-by-step way, steps can help teachers identify where student understanding is breaking down; in this way, steps can serve as an error analysis tool. Figures 3.1, 3.2, and 3.3 show sample steps for three different mathematics tasks.

1. <u>Underline</u> the word that comes after "nearest."
2. <u>Underline</u> the digit in the indicated place.
3. (Circle) the digit to the right of the <u>underlined</u> place.
4. If the circled digit is 5 or greater, add 1 to the underlined place and change all digits to the right to zeros.
5. If the circled digit is 4 or less, keep the underlined place and change all digits to the right to zeros.

Figure 3.1: Sample steps for rounding numbers.

1. Write the volume formula.
2. Find the length, width, and height.
3. Multiply.

   OR

1. Count the number of unit cubes.

Figure 3.2: Sample steps for finding the volume of a solid.

1. Rewrite in working form.
2. Multiply the ones place by the ones place (regroup if necessary).
3. Multiply the tens place by the ones place (add the regrouped digit and regroup again if necessary).
4. Continue with the hundreds place by the ones place, and so on.

Figure 3.3: Sample steps for multiplying multidigit numbers by one-digit numbers.

During the I Do It phase, students watch and listen, free from the cognitive overload of watching, listening, and learning new content while simultaneously attempting to write. Teachers often conduct the Why Do It and I Do It phases on the classroom carpet before moving to desks and tables for other parts of the lesson. This portion of the lesson is briskly paced. The goal is teacher modeling of effective thinking and problem solving. Student interaction with the teacher and with one another is minimal during this step; however, it will be critical and constant for the remainder of the lesson.

During the We Do It Together phase, the teacher solves problems that are parallel to the types of problems students will solve during the You Do It phase, this time with the students in a step-by-step manner where he or she is constantly asking students to think about their problem solving, talk to their partners about their thinking, and share their thinking with the larger group when randomly selected by the teacher. Throughout the We Do It Together phase, teachers ask questions of students, provide wait time for thinking and problem solving, ask students to share steps or answers with partners, and randomly call on students for replies. Think-pair-share with A and B partners structures student conversations. We Do It Together is a crucial stage of the lesson. Students are engaged, they are required to think and solve, and teachers gain invaluable information on students' emerging understanding to which they can provide targeted and immediate corrective feedback. In this stage, students should be talking 50 percent of the time. Teachers should ask a question first and then select a student to answer so that all students are engaged. The teacher and students solve problems together, with students taking more responsibility as the lesson proceeds. The teacher constantly checks for understanding and monitors progress to determine who is ready to move to independence. If most of the class is lacking a sufficient level of understanding, the teacher does not release responsibility; rather, the teacher extends the We Do It Together phase.

Teachers then assign students to tasks (based on their assessed readiness) to be completed in their groups during the You Do It Together phase. If some students are not ready to be released to this level of independence, teachers can use this instructional time to meet with those students in small groups to complete tasks with them in a much more guided fashion. Students who are working in groups receive instruction and support on how to work with one another to solve problems and support one another when members make errors.

The transition from the You Do It Together to the You Do It Alone phase can proceed fluidly based on student readiness. During this transition, students can present their solutions, provide the teacher with feedback on their mastery, and help cement their understanding. In addition, this strategy allows the teacher and students to build a collection of alternative ways of solving problems. If encouraged to do so, students will often solve problems in ways that are not necessarily identical to the way in which they were taught.

The phases of instruction in the gradual release of responsibility model are deductive, structured, and differentiated. More inductive lessons are also effective in mathematics. The key to success with all lessons is to focus the objective and to gradually release responsibility to students after they have received appropriate guidance on how to think and problem solve mathematically.

Making Time for Mathematics

Just as in reading and writing, students should have the opportunity to creatively and independently solve mathematics problems. Whether within the mathematics lesson, as an extension of the mathematics lesson, or as an activity students complete during independent work time, students should be given the opportunity to solve problems using models, diagrams, and computations they have learned. Strategies and steps that students have recently learned should be permanently posted and accessible at all times during these mathematics opportunities. In addition, students can be encouraged (but not required) to use the strategies described in the interventions section of the chapter (starting on page 91) during these free-response mathematics times. Open-ended, free-response mathematics prompts can be found online, including MARS (Mathematics Assessment Resource Service) tasks at www.insidemathematics.org and other task-based resources from the Silicon Valley Mathematics Initiative at www.svmimac.org.

Like reading and writing, mathematics should be an integral part of a student's day, every day. Providing students with prompts and free time in which to play with mathematics is a necessity.

Mathematics Assessment

Assessment and diagnosis in mathematics is qualitatively different than assessments and needs analyses in reading and writing. There are efficient, easy-to-administer, and easy-to-analyze universal screening measures that should be used with all students so that teachers know immediately if students are desperately at risk in mathematics. In kindergarten through third grade, universal screening can involve assessing knowledge of number and computational fluency, including areas such as number name and meaning; magnitude comparison (8 is larger than 4, 8 is larger than 6, and 6 is larger than 4); strategic counting (not simply knowledge of counting principles, but skill in counting); and solving word problems (Gersten, Jordan, & Flojo, 2005; Lembke & Foegen, 2009; Locuniak & Jordan, 2008; Mazzocco & Thompson, 2005; Methe, Hintze, & Floyd, 2008). Teacher teams can easily create brief assessments or find them online at sites such as www.interventioncentral.org or http://easycbm.com. Resources for universal screening and progress monitoring for early numeracy skills are included in the additional resources at **go.solution-tree.com/rti.**

When screening reveals that students are at risk in the areas of number sense, they must receive immediate support, even during the first month of kindergarten. Number sense is fundamental and foundational to every concept in mathematics (Buffum et al., 2012).

Although mathematics assessment has much in common with writing and reading assessment, it also differs in many respects. Disaggregating errors on formative or summative assessments can inform the teacher about student progress. This item analysis helps teams identify the domain, cluster, standard, and substandard of mathematics with which a student is struggling. As noted previously, standards often represent multiple learning targets. Specific items on a test, however, most often specifically assess a skill within a standard. When teams move beyond identification of the domain and standard with which a student is experiencing difficulty, the job of intervening becomes much clearer. In the Common Core State Standards, an example of a domain is Number and Operations in Base Ten. An example of a cluster is Understand Place Value. An example of a standard is "Understand that the three digits of a three-digit number represent amounts of hundreds, tens, and ones; for example 706 equals 7 hundreds, 0 tens, and 6 ones." An example of a substandard is, "100 can be thought of as a bundle of ten tens—called a 'hundred.'" A teacher's full understanding of standards impacts instruction and how specifically he or she can analyze student needs.

There are different options available for K–3 assessments in mathematics. Multiple-response assessments, while perhaps not as authentic as performance-based assessments and open-ended assessments, can be used for diagnosis. Often, one of the distracters in a multiple-response assessment is purposefully chosen because it represents a common error that students make. For example, if students tend to regroup incorrectly in a multidigit addition or subtraction problem, one or more of the distracters can represent such an error. Collaborative analyses of open-ended responses by teacher teams can certainly contribute significantly to diagnoses. When open-ended assessments are scored using a simple rubric that guides teachers to assess students' abilities to understand the problem, solve the problem, and answer the problem, and when these analyses are examined collaboratively, teams can discover grade-level or individual-student needs.

Teams should frequently monitor the progress of students receiving supplemental supports. Research on curriculum-based measurements in mathematics is recent, and these types of assessments are not widely available (Lembke & Stecker, 2007). Nonetheless, we now know the key areas in which progress should be monitored:

- Number identification
- Number writing
- Strategic counting
- Magnitude comparison
- Missing number
- Quantity array
- Number meaning
- Single and multidigit computation in all operations
- Word problems with all operations

The math topics examined early in this chapter represent areas in which schools may want to universally screen all students. The list above includes key areas schools may want to monitor in more specific and more numerous topics of mathematics. The additional resources at **go.solution-tree .com/rti** include several samples from each grade of mathematics progress monitoring tools. Other resources, such as http://easycbm.com, also provide ideas and tools for monitoring.

In addition to structured assessment, teachers should keep in mind that one of the most powerful assessment activities is sitting with a student for twenty minutes to listen to his or her mathematical reasoning. To do this, the teacher presents a student with a set of problems from the appropriate grade level, one at a time, and observes. The teacher frequently (for each problem) asks why and what the student is doing—particularly (but not exclusively) when mistakes are made. The knowledge gleaned from this session is invaluable—it directly informs the necessary supports for students. These one-on-one diagnostic conversations may be time consuming, but they need not be done with every student—just those students who have not responded to initial instruction and intervention.

Many educators lament that there are fewer assessments available in mathematics than in other subjects, such as reading. Diagnosing needs in mathematics is very different, however. Regardless of grade level, we can analyze student needs as generally falling within one of five domains: phonemic awareness, phonics, fluency, vocabulary, and comprehension. Learning targets in mathematics are much more specific to a grade level. Students who have deficits in number or computation are always going to be intensively at risk; in mathematics more clearly than in reading, however, we can collaboratively identify specific skills (such as regrouping when adding or subtracting) or processes (such as interpreting data) with which groups of students or individual students are struggling. Analyzing student thinking on a by-the-standard, by-the-item basis and committing to observing students who have not yet responded to instruction and intervention to determine the types of support required will ensure that every student leaves kindergarten, first grade, second grade, and third grade with mastery of grade-level content.

Mathematics Interventions

There are several current and cohesive reports that summarize best strategies for intervening in the area of mathematics (Baker et al., 2002; Gersten et al., 2008, 2009; Hattie, 2009). The following is a synthesis of the research recommendations:

- Ensure that students get specific feedback and information in their areas of need.
- Provide structured opportunities for students to talk with one another about their mathematical understanding.
- Deliver explicit, direct, and systematic instruction that includes models of proficient problem solving, verbalization of thought processes, reference to step-by-step strategies, guided practice, corrective feedback, and frequent reviews.
- Provide scaffolded opportunities for students to verbalize their understanding of math problems, starting by applying the steps to find the solution.
- Visually represent math problems.

- Focus intensively on in-depth treatment of whole numbers.

- Focus on solving word problems based on common structures.

- Devote time within each session to building computational fluency.

- Frequently and validly monitor progress.

- Include motivational strategies within instruction.

- Carefully select examples that address multiple problem types and that are presented in a logical, scaffolded manner.

- Provide general problem-solving steps and multiple strategies.

- Use ongoing formative data and feedback, combined with targeted reteaching, to immediately address gaps in understanding.

- Provide feedback to students on the impact of their effort and growth.

- Arrange for peer-to-peer supports, particularly cross-age supports.

These strategies apply to initial, core instruction as well as to interventions and represent the key elements of RTI in kindergarten through third grade. Sound core instruction should result in a low number of students later assessed as at risk. Most students who initially demonstrate misunderstandings can receive in-class support. If progress monitoring reveals that students are still not responding to instruction and intervention, then teams must provide more intensive supports.

Intervention Strategies for Small Groups

Research shows that the following interventions may be beneficial during more intensive supports (Newman-Gonchar, Clarke, & Gersten, 2009):

- **Concrete-representational-abstract (CRA) sequence (Miller & Hudson, 2007)**— In the concrete stage, the teacher models concepts with concrete materials, such as cubes, blocks, bars, or figures. In the representational stage, the teacher transitions the concrete model into a representational or semiconcrete model, using drawings, pictures, circles, dots, or tallies. In the last stage, the abstract stage, the teacher models the concept symbolically, using only numbers and mathematical notations, such as digits and operation symbols. Topics for small-group instruction may include identifying and writing numbers; identifying more, less, and equal; identifying place value; and doing addition and subtraction. The CRA sequence is also described as the 3D-to-2D-to-symbolic approach. For example, a teacher may first use cubes to represent quantities to be added, such as 4 added to 5. Next, the teacher uses boxes drawn on paper to represent the same quantities, and then finally writes the numeric and operation symbols.

- **Guess and check**—Students start by making a reasonable guess at the solution to a problem. They then apply all of the problem's "steps" to the initial guess, and check if the answer is too high or low, adjusting subsequent guesses accordingly. They use tables to organize their guesses. For example, consider the following problem: "Sophie plays 115 iPod games. Ten are animal games. The rest are word games and puzzle games. She plays twice as many word as puzzle games. How many puzzle games does she play?" Students first identify key pieces of information, repeatedly reading the problem and paraphrasing the problem. For example, "I know there are twice as many word games as puzzle games. There are 10 animal games. The total number of games is 115." Students then create a table to organize their guessing and checking, as shown in figure 3.4.

Guesses for the Number of Puzzle Games	The Number of Word Games (Twice the Number of Puzzle Games)	The Number of Animal Games (Always 10)	Total (Add the Number of Puzzle, Word, and Animal Games)	Too High or Too Low?
10	20	10	40	Too low
20	40	10	70	Too low
50	100	10	160	Too high
40	80	10	130	Too high
30	60	10	100	Too low
35	70	10	115	Correct answer!

Figure 3.4: Example of a guess-and-check problem table.

- **Create a model**—Using basic drawings, lines, or numbers, students visualize a mathematics problem. For example, "Four students were standing in line at lunch. Juliana was behind Summer. Itzel was between Juliana and Summer. Juliana was in front of Chloe. Who was the last student to receive lunch?" After reading the question to identify key information, students draw a picture that represents the problem, adding details as they reread:

  (Front of Line)—Summer—Juliana (Back of Line)

  (Front of Line)—Summer—Itzel—Juliana (Back of Line)

  (Front of Line)—Summer—Itzel—Juliana—Chloe (Back of Line)

- **Work backward**—Students first identify items represented in the problem and then perform operations in the opposite order presented. For example, "Amy brought five cupcakes home from the classroom party. Thirteen cupcakes were eaten at the party. There were twenty-two cupcakes at the beginning of the party. If Amy's teacher brought the remaining cupcakes to the teachers' lounge, how many cupcakes did she bring?" After reading the question to identify key information, students identify the total number of cupcakes: 22. Next, the number of cupcakes eaten is subtracted: 22 – 13 = 9. Finally, the number of cupcakes that Amy brought home is subtracted: 9 – 5 = 4. Amy's teacher brought 4 cupcakes to the teachers' lounge.

These are just a few research-based strategies for mathematics instruction (for others, such as the bar model, see the online resources at **go.solution-tree.com/rti**). Repeatedly and explicitly teaching these strategies to all students, and to students at risk in particular, equips students with solid strategies for solving problems that they can apply in various situations. Confidence and success with strategies leads to greater student endurance and proficiency (Ainsworth & Christinson, 2006). During intervention sessions, students should be taught the rules for each strategy. Teachers should post strategies around the classroom, and students should record them in their notebooks so they can access them independently during lessons. Teachers should model a problem using each strategy and then solve similar problems with students in an abbreviated version of the gradual release of responsibility model. Next, students should solve partially completed problems in pairs and then entire problems in pairs and individually. To enhance persistence and develop self-regulation, students should set goals, score their own work, and graph their progress.

Mathematics intervention, particularly in kindergarten through third grade, is far more a matter of prevention than supplemental supports; however, there are four additional specific ways in which teachers can support students at risk in K–3 mathematics: (1) front-loading and revisiting number sense, (2) explicitly teaching word problems, (3) providing explicit and early instruction in basic facts, and (4) transforming calendar time.

Front-Loading and Revisiting Number Sense

An analysis of traditional mathematics texts would reveal that the content covered from chapter to chapter varies a great deal from one publisher's text to the next. A similar characteristic of these texts is that number sense concepts are spread out across all chapters. As a preventative step, front-loading number sense content makes sense. As mentioned, number sense is the foundation of mathematics, much as phonological awareness is to reading (Gersten et al., 2005; Jordan, Kaplan, Olah, & Locuniak, 2006; Jordan, Kaplan, Ramineni, & Locuniak, 2009), and it is a key foundation to other subject content as well (Buffum et al., 2012). When number sense instruction occurs early in the school year, students at risk can receive supplemental supports sooner.

Explicitly Teaching Word Problems

Mathematics word problems possess a unique language and vocabulary. Many older students have developed a fear of word problems—a fear educators may have created through avoiding them in the early grades because we think of them as too difficult (National Research Council, 2001). Teacher teams in grades K–3 should explicitly teach word problems to students. One strategy is to develop operation word charts with students. These charts can help students identify the operations with key terms. An example appears in figure 3.5.

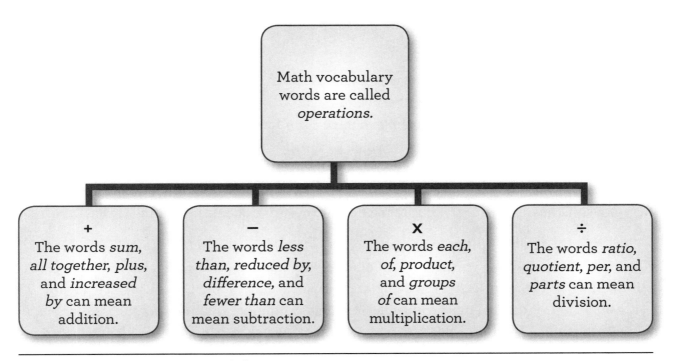

Figure 3.5: Sample operation word chart.

Teachers can also use a generic strategy such as CUBS to help students attack word problems. Using CUBS, students (1) <u>c</u>ircle numbers, in both numeral and word form; (2) <u>u</u>nderline operation words; (3) <u>b</u>ox what the question is asking them to find; and (4) <u>s</u>tate the answer, leaving a space for the ultimate solution. For example,

Ernesto sells newspapers. He sold (114) papers on Monday. He sold (78) papers on Tuesday.

What is the <u>total</u> amount of newspapers Ernesto sold? Ernesto sold a total of _____

newspapers, or the sum of newspapers that Ernesto sold was _____.

Providing Explicit and Early Instruction in Basic Facts

The most profound way in which mathematics and mathematics intervention in kindergarten through third grade should be changed is with more explicit and robust instruction in basic facts.

Teachers should start with a simple but rigorous and non-negotiable expectation: students will demonstrate mastery of math facts in all operations, including in multidigit applications, by the end of third grade. Teachers and students should consistently employ the commutative property when mastering math facts. The commutative property applies to addition and multiplication and signifies that the terms in addition and multiplication problems can be reversed: 6 + 7 = 7 + 6 and 6 × 7 = 7 × 6. Therefore, when introducing the sum of 2 + 3, teachers will always introduce 3 + 2 (Slavin & Lake, 2008). When introducing 5 × 6, teachers will always introduce 6 × 5. While many teachers teach the commutative property and fact families within textbook-based lessons, teachers have not consistently employed fact families in their efforts to ensure students master math facts in addition and multiplication.

In addition, the only way in which teachers should teach subtraction facts is through addition facts, and the only way in which teachers should teach division facts is through multiplication facts (Swun, 2011). For example, when introducing a subtraction fact, a teacher would prompt students with, "Since 2 + 3 = 5, then 5 – 2 = 3 and 5 – 3 = 2." When introducing a multiplication fact, teachers would prompt students with, "Since 5 × 6 = 30, then 30 ÷ 5 = 6 and 30 ÷ 6 = 5." Again, while teachers occasionally make students aware of fact families in textbook-based lessons, they have not consistently used fact families in efforts to ensure students master math facts.

Finally, in the same mini-lesson in which a few facts are introduced (for example, 2 + 3 and 3 + 2, as well as 2 + 4 and 4 + 2), students should be expected to apply these facts in multidigit situations. Thus, in the mini-lesson involving the sample facts, multidigit problems may include 23 + 42 and 32 + 24. Students must apply new learning in multiple and more complex situations to truly learn (Bull & Johnston, 1997). When the application of facts requires students to regroup, teachers should precede such instruction with a brief mini-lesson. Regrouping need not be a significant hurdle; the likelihood that regrouping will present difficulties is lessened when students are consistently asked to apply new facts to solve multidigit problems.

Students should receive explicit instruction in math facts beginning as early as kindergarten (Wurman & Wilson, 2012). Schools should consider identifying the following key content and expectations for mastery (Swun, 2011):

- Students master sums to ten by the end of kindergarten.
- Students master addition, including addition of multidigit whole numbers and money, by the end of first grade.
- Students master subtraction, including subtraction of multidigit whole numbers and money, by the end of second grade.

- Students master multiplication and division, including the multiplication and division of multidigit whole numbers by digits (with money), by the end of third grade.

When educators focus on breadth over depth, they risk denying students the opportunity to master key content in favor of learning mere facts. There are important concepts and procedures that teachers should explicitly teach to students in the early grades as students are acquiring math facts. These critical prerequisites include:

- Knowledge and concept of numbers 1–100 through picture representations, use of manipulatives, tally marks, and so on

- One-to-one correspondence

- Conservation of number

- Knowledge and concept of addition through picture representations, use of manipulatives, tally marks, and so on

- The 0 and 1 rules of addition

- Knowledge of symbols used in simple number sentence or equations (such as $2 + 3 = 5$)

The solution may be to front-load kindergarten and first-grade students with these prerequisite skills early in the year, consistently reinforcing and applying them during explicit instruction of math facts throughout the year.

When providing explicit math instruction to students in a systematically scoped and sequenced manner, teachers give students multiple opportunities to write, say, and hear facts, both individually, with their classmates, and with the teacher. The same gradual release of responsibility model that teachers use in all effective instruction should be used when helping students master math facts.

In the early grades, teachers often believe that students have already acquired mastery of math facts. Teachers should keep in mind that mastery does not mean using fingers, tally marks, or other useful heuristics. Students should use these strategies only until mastery has been established. However, mastery does not mean that students can, if given sufficient time, produce the correct fact. Mastery or computational fluency means that students can produce facts with automaticity. In the absence of automatic and confident mastery of facts, the cognitive load that students are forced to dedicate to basic computation will negatively affect their effort to master more complex mathematical problem solving.

While computational automaticity and fluency with whole numbers from 0 to 9 in all four operations by the end of third grade is an absolute necessity, a conceptual understanding of numbers is critical. Teachers and students should engage in meaningful lessons that solidify students' representational awareness of addition, subtraction, multiplication, and division. Through visual and concrete reinforcements, students should understand that addition implies grouping together, subtraction implies taking away from, multiplication implies multiple addition or adding equally sized groups, and division implies separating into equally sized groups.

Although this conceptual understanding of mathematics is essential, students must master math facts as well. Conceptual and procedural understandings are equally important (Rittle-Johnson et al., 2001; Wurman & Wilson, 2012). Math facts instruction should occur in addition to core math instruction. Schools should schedule another twenty to thirty minutes of supplemental time daily for mathematics instruction that focuses on the automatic mastery of math facts.

Transforming Calendar Time

Teachers and students in primary grades usually have a tradition of meeting on the carpet some time at the beginning of the day to build community and engage in consistent, repetitive, and productive tasks. This "calendar time" has been eliminated in some buildings in an effort to eliminate non-standards-based instruction. However, calendar time, when focused on key math content, can actually represent a powerful community-building and content-building feature of daily classroom life. The likelihood of students mastering key content is greatly increased when it is built into classroom routines and embedded within real-life procedures.

Table 3.4 lists standards from kindergarten through grade 3 along with sample calendar activities that teachers can introduce progressively across grade levels with an increase in complexity and rigor. The repetition in addressing key content provides necessary reinforcement and support for students.

While students in kindergarten and first grade may still sit on the carpet for calendar time, second- and third-grade students may have graduated from this routine. Nonetheless, the simple tasks identified in table 3.4 can contribute mathematically rich content to the routines of each day.

The Four Questions of RTI in Mathematics

Teacher teams and schoolwide teams should regularly consider the following four questions when determining whether students are responding to instruction and intervention (Buffum et al., 2012):

Table 3.4: Sample Calendar Time Activities Based on the CCSS

Kindergarten Skills	First-Grade Skills	Second-Grade Skills	Third-Grade Skills	Sample Calendar Activities

• Know number names and counting
• Count the number of objects in a set
• Compare the number of objects in a set
• Add (put together or add to) and subtract (take apart or take from)
• Understand place value
• Classify objects and count the number of objects in categories
• Identify, describe, analyze, compare, create, and compose shapes
	• Solve problems involving addition and subtraction
	• Count the number of objects in larger sets
	• Understand place value
	• Tell and write time
	• Represent and interpret data
	• Reason with shapes and their attributes
		• Solve problems involving addition and subtraction
		• Work with equal groups as the foundation for multiplication
		• Understand place value
		• Work with time and money
		• Represent and interpret data
		• Reason with shapes and their attributes
			• Solve problems involving the four operations
			• Use place value
			• Develop understanding of fractions as numbers
			• Represent and interpret data
			• Reason with shapes and their attributes
				• Practice 1-to-1 correspondence (use realia, tally marks, pictures)
				• Use hundreds chart for the first 100 days of school:
				  + Match to base-10 blocks
				  + Identify before, between, after
				  + Start at different points (start counting at 10 or 45 instead of always at 1
				  + Count backwards
				  + Skip count by 2s, 5s, and 10s, periodically starting at different points
				  + Reinforce place value
				• Identify days of the week and months of the year
				• Identify colors and color patterns, in combination with the hundreds chart, shapes, and calendar
				• Identify plane and solid shapes of various sizes and orientations
				• Identify sets with greater, less, or equal amounts
				• Identify coins, their values, and combinations
				• Tell time to the hour, half-hour, and quarter-hour
				• Write the fraction/ratio for the number of days in the month, the number of girls (or boys), and the number of students in the class

Source: NGA & CCSSO, 2010b.

1. **About which students do we have concerns?** Mathematics screening can occur early in the school year in grades K–3 so that supports can be immediately provided. The primary areas in which screeners should be administered are number name and meaning, magnitude comparison, strategic counting, and word problems, in addition to math facts.

2. **In what areas do we have concerns?** Areas of mathematical need can be much more efficiently diagnosed than needs in reading, writing, or English language. By analyzing errors at the standard-level and item-level, and ultimately by engaging in one-on-one, teacher-to-student dialogues on solving specific problems, teachers can identify and address the needs of individual students.

3. **What are we currently doing to support the student and meet the student's needs?** In addition to the simple, but important responding to item-level and root-cause analyses manner of ameliorating the mathematics needs of students, there are other supports that all teams of teacher must consider for their repertoire: (1) explicitly teaching and repeatedly practicing intervention strategies such as concrete, representational-abstract (CRA), guess-and-check, creating a model, and working backward; (2) front-loading and revisiting number sense; (3) explicitly teaching word problems; (4) providing explicit and early instruction in basic facts; and (5) transforming calendar time.

4. **Has the student responded to the instruction and interventions (the supports) that we have been providing?** Teachers can monitor the progress of students at risk in mathematics using the same measures used for screening, as long as they are new, alternate versions. When teacher teams have identified student needs through the analysis of common formative assessments, student progress should be monitored by asking that they later demonstrate their mastery on tasks similar to those on the original common formative assessment, after they have received additional reteaching and support.

Summary

The performance of U.S. students in mathematics has been judged to be subpar. If we are committed to securing success for students, we must be committed to thinking and acting differently. In the area of mathematics, this entails a focus on depth over breadth, sequencing number sense earlier in the school year, and raising expectations for the rigor of content that students can master, beginning but not ending with automaticity with operations. Schools can achieve previously unknown levels of student success in math when educators rethink mathematics instruction for students in kindergarten through third grade to focus on the building of essential skills and the prevention of future deficiencies. Use the reproducible Guiding Goals for K–3 Mathematics checklist (page 102) to help determine the next steps you will take (in your classroom, team, school, or district) in your RTI-based K–3 program.

The next chapter will describe effective supports for English learners. Just like reading, writing, and mathematics, supports for English learners must be based on balanced research and must be integrated into core instruction and occur all day long.

Guiding Goals for K–3 Mathematics

Goal	Long-Term Vision	First Steps
Unpack standards and focus instruction	Staff study state standards and the CCSS, unpack the standards to build consensus on rigor and format, and design a focused scope and sequence of mathematics instruction.	☐ Staff collaboratively unpack state and CCSS. ☐ Staff collaboratively study research, such as the findings summarized by the National Mathematics Advisory Panel. ☐ Teacher teams determine essentials, using tools and protocols such as those suggested by Doug Reeves and Larry Ainsworth. ☐ Teams unpack essentials using the essential standards chart.
Commit to computational fluency	Staff set the expectation, and provide the explicit instruction, to ensure that all students exit third grade with 100 percent computational fluency with all four operations, with multidigit numbers (single-digit divisors and one single-digit factor).	☐ Staff collaboratively study best practices in acquiring math facts. ☐ Staff align and focus instruction, beginning with explicit addition instruction in kindergarten.
Refine and study effective lessons, structures, and strategies	Teacher teams collaboratively study teaching, including how to structure lessons.	☐ Every teacher provides explicit instruction, with teacher metacognitive modeling, in a gradual release of responsibility format. ☐ Teachers ensure that time for small-group learning is included in lessons, while other students work independently on differentiated tasks. ☐ Teachers plan regular (at least quarterly) lesson studies in which teachers co-plan, co-teach, and co-review lessons in one another's classroom.

CHAPTER 4

English Learners

*Language shapes the way we think, and determines
what we can think about.*

BENJAMIN LEE WHORF

By many different measures, English learners are at risk and underserved in U.S. schools. On assessments of English language arts and mathematics, they underperform their English-only peers. English learners fail to meet reading and math proficiency standards on the NAEP at four times the rate of non-English learners, and gaps are increasing (California Department of Education, n.d.; National Center for Education Statistics [NCES], 2010). When examining the rates and pace at which these students are redesignated from English learner to English proficient, we find students who stall at intermediate levels of proficiency, students who do not redesignate after over a decade of support, and students who are redesignated but whose academic English is not conventional enough to pass the most basic college-entry examinations (NCES, 2010; Scarcella, 2003).

English language development is complex, and educators often disagree about how best to teach and support English learners. There is a debate between structured immersion and systematic, explicit instruction in English. Some think that a second language is acquired in the same way as a first language (Krashen & Terrell, 1983) so immersion is best, and others think it ought to be systematically and explicitly taught (McLaughlin, 1985). Both strategies are sound, but neither in isolation will allow schools to ensure high levels of learning for all students learning English as a second language.

If a student is experiencing difficulty in reading, writing, or mathematics, proficiency with the English language may be a contributing factor, or it may not. Educators must not allow "English learner" to be just another label that results in a one-size-fits-all program or approach. At-risk English learners who are not yet proficient must be diagnosed just like English-proficient students, but in addition, there are other variables to consider for core instruction, assessment, and intervention.

Research on Acquiring English

Schools face major challenges when seeking to improve the success of English learners. As Deborah Short and Shannon Fitzsimmons (2007) report, schools must overcome the following:

- A lack of assessments for identifying needs, determining proficiency levels, and monitoring progress
- Inadequate teacher training and knowledge
- A lack of appropriate and flexible programs and instructional models
- Inadequate use of effective practices
- A lack of rigorous and coherent research

These challenges are similar to those educators face in their efforts to teach reading, writing, and mathematics. A difference is that educators may not be as aware of the challenges or as ready to embrace solutions in regard to English learners.

Another important report (August & Shanahan, 2006) cites the following conclusions about English language instruction:

- Explicit and comprehensive reading instruction benefits English learners.
- Explicit and comprehensive reading instruction is necessary but not sufficient for ensuring that English learners read and write proficiently in English—oral proficiency is critical as well, but it is often overlooked.
- Proficiency and literacy in a student's primary language supports proficiency and literacy in English.
- English learners are individual students first—they have significant differences in strengths and needs.
- Assessments for English learners are weak.
- Proficiency in a student's home language positively impacts literacy.

Research in RTI (Buffum, Mattos, & Weber, 2009, 2012) has consistently advocated better core supports for English learners; core, Tier 1 supports are most critical. We must provide more explicit supports for English learners throughout all content areas. Moreover, when students are not adequately responding to core instruction, we must diagnose their needs and prescribe appropriate, targeted supports. If it is determined that a school's core, differentiated English language supports are sufficient, and yet a student's acquisition of English is delayed, then the school must provide interventions in the area of English language. If the core, differentiated English language and reading supports are sufficient and a student's acquisition of English is on pace, but the student's reading progression is inadequate, then the school must provide interventions in the area of reading. Instructional, differentiation, and intervention practices as they relate to English learners are entirely consistent with the fundamentals and foundations of RTI.

Reading instruction and intervention for English learners is often delayed or distorted because educators inappropriately connect reading skills with English language proficiency. English learners share more similarities with non-English learners than differences; English learners who are at risk in reading require the same supports as non-English learners. Of course, English learners will also require English language acquisition instruction, and perhaps, intervention. Both groups of students require scaffolds to access content, as well as early, explicit, and intensive instruction in phonological awareness and phonics to build their decoding skills (Francis, Rivera, Lesaux, Kieffer, & Rivera, 2006). These supports should not be delayed because schools attribute deficiencies in early reading skills to delays in acquiring oral language. That may or may not be the case. This is particularly relevant for English learners in kindergarten through third grade.

Equally as important, if English learners are developing phonological awareness and phonics at a normal rate, they need not receive interventions in these areas simply because they are English learners; the critical point is that neither initial, differentiated instruction nor explicit, intensive intervention (if students do not adequately respond to initial instruction) should be delayed while students are acquiring the English language. If students in kindergarten through third grade are not progressing adequately in their acquisition of the English language (increasing approximately one proficiency level per year in school while speaking English), then they should also receive supplemental supports and interventions in the forms and functions of the English language, in addition to the core instruction they receive.

Schools must also increase opportunities for K–3 English learners to develop academic vocabulary, another goal not limited to English learners but applicable to all students in the early grades (Francis et al., 2006). Vocabulary instruction cannot simply occur during English language development instruction; it must be embedded throughout all content areas. The instruction must focus on tier 1, 2, and 3 vocabulary (Beck, McKeown, & Kucan, 2002). The first tier includes basic words (*desk, bathroom*) that will not likely require explicit instruction. The second tier includes highly represented words found in multiple content areas (*coincidence, analyze*) that require explicit instruction. The third tier includes less-frequently represented words (*Fahrenheit, democracy*) found in specific content areas; while important, these words would be most efficiently taught as needed within instruction in the specific content. Simply labeling words with the images they represent is not sufficient; in addition to word identification, English learners must also develop conceptual and contextual knowledge of words. They must be able to use the words in academic settings. Instruction must also focus on how different types of words are related, through roots and affixes, and by connections to antonyms and synonyms. Idiomatic words, homonyms, and homophones must also be a focus. Finally, vocabulary instruction must be integrated into all types of tasks—whether oral or written, individual or group—and students must be equipped with strategies to determine the meaning of words on their own.

Instruction in comprehension for English learners is particularly critical in kindergarten through third grade because students gradually acquire English during this time (Francis et al., 2006). Instruction must involve narrative and expository texts and must place at least as much emphasis on the process of making meaning of texts as on products of mastery. Educators must use caution when concluding that English learners' fluency is adequate because their words correct per minute falls within the normal range; all students, but particularly English learners, may have poor comprehension despite an adequate rate. Other aspects of fluency—accuracy and expression—are just as important as rate for English learners. These aspects can be improved through increased exposure to rich vocabulary and texts. This can be accomplished with texts at English learners' instructional and independent reading levels and through repeated readings of passages—strategies that are also completely appropriate for non-English learners.

Practice with oral and written expression is critical for all students in all content areas and at all grade levels (Francis et al., 2006). For English learners in particular, opportunities for practicing oral and written expression must be frequent and structured. In order to develop both oral and written language, teachers will most likely need to provide frames based on the forms and functions of English (Dutro & Moran, 2003). Functions are universal across languages; specific grammatical forms are associated with specific functions and are unique to different languages. When instruction in English language acquisition is organized around functions and forms, meaning making is more authentic and language acquisition is functional.

Chapter 3 described the most effective instruction and interventions for students in kindergarten through third grade in mathematics. The recommendations in that chapter are even more critical for English learners. Like all primary-grade students, English learners require explicit and intensive instruction and intervention in number sense (Francis et al., 2006). Mathematics vocabulary is unique, and English learners' difficulties in mathematics may be most attributable to confusion with language. This is particularly true with word problems and when communicating solutions, either orally or in writing.

Proficiency and Transformative Pedagogy

As educators are serving more English learners than ever before, the definition of *proficiency* has grown more complex (Canale & Swain, 1980; Cummins, 1986; Kern, 2000; Kinsella, 2005). Proficiency can be defined as a native-like aptitude in listening, speaking, reading, and writing across multiple content and discourse types, so that college and career readiness is possible and probable. In preservice training, many educators learn about proficiency and about meeting the needs of English learners through the foundational work of Jim Cummins (1986) and Stephen

Krashen (1985). Their research and recommendations are fundamentally important and influential; however, interpretations and implementation of the work of Cummins and Krashen have resulted in models for serving English learners that are only partially complete and somewhat successful. Misinterpretation or partial interpretation of their work has caused schools to fall short of ensuring that all English learners are proficient in English and thus in all content areas.

Cummins (1986) notes that the actual strategies and programs used to support students are no more significant than the school's culture and climate and the level of expectations. Among other pertinent points, Cummins notes the following:

- Conversational fluency (basic interpersonal communication skills, or BICS) is not a good indicator of academic literacy in English.

- Premature exit from language supports will likely result in illiteracy in multiple languages.

- Most of the elementary school years will be required for bilingual students to bridge the gap.

- Bilingual students' acquisition of conversational fluency and academic literacy in English is not compromised if they develop academic skills in their primary language.

- Bilingualism positively impacts academic development in first and second languages.

In short, English learners possess assets that contribute to their success. Bilingualism is not a deficit.

Cummins' contributions to linguistics and his debunking of the myths of the dangers of bilingualism are profound, but perhaps the most inspiring element of his research is his advocacy for transformative pedagogy. If educators want to ensure that students attain proficiency in English and all content areas as quickly as possible, they should start by caring for and honoring students and their cultural and linguistic assets. Placing value on native languages and cultures with pedagogy in the classroom and respect throughout the school is imperative (Cummins, 1986; Lee & Oxelson, 2006; Lucas & Katz, 1994; Snow & Katz, 2010).

Like Cummins, Krashen (1985) has contributed several influential concepts to the study of second-language acquisition:

- Acquisition of language is a subconscious process, similar to the process that children undergo when learning their native language. It requires meaningful interactions, during which teachers help students focus on meaning, not just form. Learning is a conscious process in which new knowledge or forms are explicitly taught, and learning is less effective than acquisition.

- Speaking in the target language does not result in language acquisition. Output is the result of language acquisition. If teachers provide enough comprehensible input, students will naturally learn.

- A student's background knowledge acts as a monitor to what they learn and produce. Students self-monitor before speaking and self-correct after speaking. Self-monitoring and self-correction are the only functions of conscious language learning. Because adults have more background knowledge, they may learn at faster rates.

- Affective filters will impede learning or acquisition because of negative emotional responses due to anxiety, self-doubt, or boredom. These negatives act as a filter between the speaker and the listener that reduces the amount of language input the listener is able to understand. Not respecting an English learner's initial silent period and correcting errors too early raise anxieties.

Many teachers recognize Krashen's influence through two critical and related concepts: (1) students can only learn when input (instruction or content) is comprehensible, meaning we must use scaffolds and strategies to ensure students can access the curriculum; and (2) students can only learn when their anxieties are low (low affective filters), meaning the relationships we foster and the environments in which we teach and learn must be respectful.

Misapplication of research related to language supports has contributed to an overemphasis on input with low affective filters, which has unfortunately led to less direct teaching of English functions and forms and an inadequate quantity and quality of corrective feedback (Dutro & Moran, 2003; Scarcella, 2003); output must be comprehensible as well (Swain, 1985), and a focus on the language that English learners produce will help round out research and practice.

Comprehensive Supports

Robin Scarcella (2003) cites two main weaknesses among the English learner college students she studies and serves: (1) their limited vocabulary and word usage results in misuse of words and incorrect diction; and (2) their limited understanding of word forms and sentence structure results in misuse of articles, pronouns, nouns, and verb tenses (Scarcella, 1996). Too much focus on input has not served English learners whose output is too often insufficiently developed. The mission of educators should be to ensure high levels of learning for all students—learning that will allow students to graduate high school ready for college or a skilled career. For English learners, this includes becoming proficient in the English language, which involves a focus on input and output.

Educators must ensure that English learners can successfully access content in reading, mathematics, science, social studies, art, physical education, technology, and so on, for which instruction is typically provided in English. Schools cannot wait until an English learner is proficient in

English before providing content for which there are high expectations for mastery. This raises the question of how educators can ensure that students can successfully access and master content knowledge while not yet proficient in English. One approach is Specially Designed Academic Instruction in English, or SDAIE. SDAIE includes strategies and supports that will be more fully described later in the chapter. It involves instruction that ensures explicit content and language connections.

Form, Function, and Fluency

If the first task in teaching English learners is to scaffold access to content knowledge, the second task is to help them gain proficiency in the English language. Susan Dutro and Carol Moran (2003) note that to effectively attain proficiency with both the receptive (listening and reading) and expressive (speaking and writing) components of English, students need to master the grammatical forms of the language. All languages have forms. In English class, students learn the names and rules of the forms of language. To develop proficiency with the English language, English learners need to also learn how the forms sound, what they look like, how to say them properly, and how to write them correctly. Students need explicit instruction in these forms in a dedicated instruction block (Norris & Ortega, 2006; Saunders, Foorman, & Carlson, 2006; Saunders & Goldenberg, 2010), and English language development must be its own content area (Snow & Katz, 2010). Scarcella (1996) emphasizes the importance of academic English, suggesting that it has a stronger-than-sometimes-recognized connection to more informal English and suggests that modeling and explicit practice with academic English is beneficial, even essential, to students acquiring proficiency in English.

While languages are likely to have unique grammatical forms (the way verbs, nouns, reflexive elements, modifiers, and prepositions are organized), the purposes, or functions, are universal across languages. Most importantly, there are predictable, teachable, and learnable forms associated with different functions. When we compare physical characteristics or the causes of an event (examples of different language functions), we use a series of predictable grammatical forms. Educators often provide these predictable forms to students through the scaffold of sentence frames. When we systematically teach students these grammatical forms and the specific language related to the forms in the context of comprehensible, familiar functions, students' proficiency with English improves. When equipped with grammatical forms that have the utility to serve specific functions, English learners have not simply learned vocabulary words, they have learned how to use vocabulary words.

Dutro and Moran (2003) also emphasize the importance of fluency. While English learners may have many opportunities with the receptive elements of English, they do not have nearly enough opportunities with the expressive elements of English. Structuring and scaffolding opportunities for students to practice using the language, developing their oral and written fluency, is a critical component of English language development.

Key English Language Content

English language development must be its own content area directly taught during a dedicated time of day, what Dutro and Moran (2003) call "a vertical slice of the curriculum" (p. 3). They note that it must follow a developmental scope and sequence of language skills that build from simple to complex structures within the context of a range of everyday and academic language functions. In addition, English language development must be present all day, with teachers providing scaffolds so that students can access content, what Dutro and Moran call "a horizontal slice of the curriculum, across all content areas" (p. 3). During the vertical slice, language is the focus and content is in the background; during the horizontal slices, content is in the foreground, but teachers recognize and address language demands in the background.

If English language development is considered its own content area, then it should have essential standards that guide instruction. The national standards for primary grades written by the Teachers of English of Speakers of Other Languages (TESOL, 1997) provide coherence and guidance. The World-Class Instructional Design and Assessment standards (WIDA, n.d.) are similarly worthwhile. The state with more English learners than any other state, California, also has a coherent and useful set of standards for English language development. English learners make up a greater percentage of students in California than in any other state, and California has served a significant population of English learners for decades. (At the time of this writing, the California Department of Education is in the process of revising its ELD standards.) Table 4.1 provides a synthesis and summary of the TESOL and California standards for primary grades. In terms of standards-based instruction, English language development is behind most other content areas. This must change if we are to improve the supports we provide to English learners.

Dutro, Prestridge, and Jeanne Herrick (2005) have developed a matrix of grammatical forms that can help educators determine which language frames to explicitly teach students, as well as the progression that students take as they move from beginning to advanced in their English language development. Samples from the matrix appear in table 4.2 (page 112). The matrix is intended to help teachers organize and sequence instruction. English learners must be able to use language, and the grammatical forms listed in the matrix are the tools they need to use both orally and in writing. When teachers collaboratively reflect on and analyze students' proficiency with oral and written expression, they should determine whether students are using the different forms (such as verbs, pronouns, adjectives, and prepositions) of language correctly. More specifically and diagnostically, teacher should identify the proficiency levels at which students are using the different forms and target instruction on these forms at those levels. A matrix such as the one in table 4.2 can assist teachers in this diagnostic-prescriptive process. During English language instruction, teachers need not "name" the parts of speech and students need not identify the differences (for example, between adjectives and adverbs). That's the domain of teachers in the content area of English language arts.

Table 4.1: Synthesis and Summary of TESOL's National Standards and California's English Language Development Standards

English learners will be able to proficiently . . .	
• Ask and answer questions	• Recognize English phonemes that do not correspond to sounds that students hear and produce
• Behave appropriately in response to cues	
• Compare and contrast	• Recognize words that have multiple meanings
• Comprehend nonverbal cues and body language	• Rehearse language for use in different settings
• Conduct transactions	• Represent information visually
• Describe a favorite activity	• Respond to and use humor appropriately
• Determine appropriate topics for interaction	• Retell familiar stories and short conversations using gestures, expressions, and illustrations
• Draw and label pictures related to a story or experiences	
• Experiment with language in social and academic settings	• Seek assistance, support, and feedback from adults and peers
• Explain actions	• Select different media to help understand language
• Express preferences and needs	• Self-monitor language use in various settings and with various audiences
• Focus attention selectively	
• Follow oral and written directions	• Share and request information
• Gather information	• Speak comprehensibly using standard English grammatical forms, sounds, intonation, pitch, and modulation
• Learn and use language chunks	
• Listen to and imitate others using English	
• Negotiate and initiate conversations	• Understand and produce academic vocabulary
• Identify the basic sequence of events in text read aloud	• Understand and use idiomatic expressions
• Participate in full class, group, and pair discussions	• Use common English morphemes to derive meaning in oral and silent reading
• Persuade, negotiate, evaluate, and justify	• Use context to make meaning
• Predict and infer	• Use native language resources appropriately
• Produce English phonemes that correspond to phonemes that students already hear and produce	• Use slang appropriately
	• Use the appropriate formal register
	• Use the primary language to ask for clarification
• Recognize appropriate ways of speaking for various purposes, audiences, and subject matters	• Write appropriately for different audiences, purposes, and settings

Source: TESOL, 1997, 2006; and California Department of Education, 2002.

Table 4.2: Sample Forms From the Matrix of Grammatical Forms

Grammatical Forms	Intermediate Forms
Verbs: Describing actions and states of being	Negative present and past progressive (were not walking)
	Present perfect (has been)
	Imperatives (Stop doing that, please.)
Nouns and articles: Naming people, places, and things	Uncountable nouns (some)
	Possessive nouns (teacher's)
	Collective nouns (bunch of kids)
Pronouns: Renaming people, places, and things	Demonstrative pronouns (*Those* are mine.)
	Possessive pronouns (*my/mine*)
Prepositions: Connecting ideas	Location (*on* the left)
	Direction (toward)
	Time (*in* April)
Conjunctions: Connecting ideas	To explain (because)
	To contrast (but)
	To show cause or effect (so)
Adjectives: Describing what kind, how many, how much, and which one	Comparative/superlative (good/better/best)
	Multi (*dry, brown* soil)
	Demonstrative (*This* book)
Adverbs: Describing when, where, how, and why	Without -ly (well)
	To describe frequency (always)
	Modify adjective (*very* late)

Source: Dutro, Prestridge, and Herrick, 2005; and E. L. Achieve, 2006. Reprinted with permission.

The matrix also helps educators specify the verb forms that are so critical to English learners as they progressively express themselves with more competence, confidence, and clarity. Lack of fluency with verb forms both limits English learners' flexibility when using the language and reveals their lack of proficiency. Dutro and Carol Maron's progression of verb forms and simple samples are briefly summarized in table 4.3 (Dutro & Moran, 2003).

Table 4.3: Progression of Verb Forms for English Learners (From Less Advanced to More Advanced)

Verb Form	Example
Present progressive tense	Is walking; is not walking
Past progressive tense	Was walking; was not walking
Future tense	Going to walk
Present perfect tense	*Have/has* plus past participle: She has been walking a mile each day for the past year.
Phrasal verbs	Walk down the street; walk up the path
Past perfect tense	*Had* plus past participle: We hadn't been walking long.
Conditional form	If we walk to the store, we will not be able to carry many bags.
Future and conditional perfect tenses	Has been walking; will have been walking; If she had walked, she would have gotten some exercise.
Passive voice	It was written by . . . ; this picture was taken by my grandfather.

Source: Dutro & Moran, 2003.

Determining the content that comprises a systematic, explicit English language development program is only the first step. Scoping and sequencing key content to ensure that students acquire English is the next step.

English Language Instruction

Before examining effective instructional strategies, it is wise to identify how educators define the proficiency levels of English learners. The number of levels varies from five to six. Table 4.4 (page 114) synthesizes English learners' proficiency in five levels as defined by TESOL (2006) and the California Department of Education (2002). As noted previously, there are more English learners in California than in any other state, and English learners make up a greater percentage of students in California than in any other state; moreover, this phenomenon has been a reality in California for decades. There are two labels provided for each of the five levels. The first is used by TESOL and the second by the California Department of Education.

There are two primary reasons to know the language proficiency levels of students. First, students should be grouped by proficiency level or proficiency band during their explicit English language development block, even if this necessitates that adjacent grade levels be combined. While

Table 4.4: English Language Proficiency Levels

Level 1: Starting or Beginning	Level 2: Emerging or Early Intermediate	Level 3: Developing or Intermediate	Level 4: Expanding or Early Advanced	Level 5: Bridging or Advanced
English language learners can . . .				
• Communicate with others around basic concrete needs, with frequent errors • Use and understand high-frequency words and memorized language • Understand nonverbal representations of language • Have limited receptive English skills • Express themselves in a limited manner orally and in writing	• Communicate with others using language that draws on routine experiences • Use and understand high-frequency words and general academic vocabulary • Produce oral or written language with errors that impede meaning • Have more developed receptive and productive English skills • Express themselves orally and in writing with phrases, memorized statements, and questions	• Communicate with others on familiar matters • Use and understand general and some specialized academic vocabulary • Produce oral or written language with errors that do not detract from the meaning • Tailor English skills to meet communication and learning demands • Express themselves orally and in writing with sentences, paragraphs, original statements, and questions	• Communicate in both concrete and abstract situations and apply language to new experiences • Use and understand specialized and some technical academic vocabulary • Use a variety of sentence lengths and complexity in oral and written communication • Produce oral and written language, with errors that do not impede meaning • Combine the elements of English in complex, cognitively demanding situations • Express themselves orally and in writing with more elaborate discourse, fully developed paragraphs, and compositions	• Communicate on a range of longer texts and recognize implicit meaning • Use and understand technical academic vocabulary • Use a variety of sentence lengths and complexity in extended oral or written communication • Produce oral or written language comparably with English-proficient peers • Respond in English using academic vocabulary in social and academic settings to negotiate meaning

Source: TESOL, 2006.

teachers may specifically identify students' current proficiency as existing at one of five levels, it is also common to target instruction and group students in proficiency bands—levels 1–2 in one group, level 3 in one group, and levels 4–5 in one group. One might question grouping English learners by proficiency level or proficiency band for instruction in English because it would seem to remove language models from the classroom. However, English learners may not feel secure enough to produce language with peers who possess higher levels of proficiency. Thus, the teacher should be the model.

The second purpose of proficiency levels is to differentiate content, process, product, and questioning for English learners within content area instruction. While all students will be expected to achieve mastery of content area standards, teachers can increase English learners' success by differentiating the way in which they access content (for example, with redacted readings); the process by which content is studied (for example, with visual supports and heterogeneous groupings); the products that represent student mastery (such as visuals, graphic organizers, and PowerPoints); and the types of questions they ask students and the ways in which students answer.

Instruction must ensure that students learn at high levels, but English learners also need engaging approaches to access content areas and become proficient in English. The following section examines best practices for ensuring students successfully access content.

Sheltered Instruction

Teachers must use effective strategies for scaffolding subject-area content so that English learners can be successful. These strategies, known as sheltered instruction or SDAIE, must be purposeful, planned, and consistently employed; the accidental sheltered instruction that sometimes occurs in classrooms is not adequate (Moughamian, Rivera, & Francis, 2009). Sheltered instructional strategies include the following:

- Cooperative learning environments in which students have opportunities to work and learn from other students and engage in a variety of modes of interacting with content, including student to student, student to teacher, student to text, and student to self, through reflection and self-evaluation

- Thematic learning environments in which common threads and standards from multiple subject areas, such as English language arts, science, and social studies, are interwoven and explicit connections are made; in these environments, teachers identify the most essential learning targets between content areas so that the breadth of content is reduced, allowing students more time to master essentials and more opportunities for depth

- Scaffolding that includes constant connection to prior learning, rephrasing, and paraphrasing; graphic organizers that display and process information; teacher-determined instruction of prerequisite standards and identified processes toward mastery of standards; prereading and rereading activities; previews of vocabulary with pictorial supports; listening and speaking activities that precede reading and writing activities; the use of realia, props, and manipulatives by students throughout the lesson; and teachers who actively acquire a wealth of knowledge on students so they can constantly connect learning to students' experiences and knowledge

- Lesson designs within units that are appropriately paced with metacognitive and self-regulatory (or, executive functioning) strategies that are explicitly modeled; there is an expectation and the opportunity to engage in higher-order critical thinking skills; the environment, instruction, and materials are predictable; and routines reduce anxieties and the mystery about how learning will occur

- Checks for understanding (including informal assessments) that are made constantly, not just to assess progress toward mastery but also to ensure that students understand teacher input so that learning can begin

- Validation of diversity so that all students, experiences, and languages are publicly valued

Sheltered instruction does not imply that standards are watered down or that expectations are lower; expectations do not change, but teachers recognize that the level of supports needed to achieve high levels of learning may be different and perhaps greater than with native English speakers.

A popular research-based method of sheltering instruction is Guided Language Acquisition Design (known as Project GLAD). Project GLAD includes professional development, unit planning, and instructional models. Teachers use specific instructional and management strategies that promote positive learning environments. The classroom environments created are orally and visually rich in language and pictorial supports, and students constantly interact, participate, and practice. Teachers heavily emphasize the use of academic vocabulary, and students use frames and stems to allow for effective communication. Classroom environments value the student, provide authentic opportunities for the use of academic language, and maintain the highest standards and expectations. The concept of "teach to the highest" is paramount, and authentic opportunities for use of academic language are constant. Writing receives heavy emphasis.

The Sheltered Instruction Observation Protocol (SIOP) from the Center for Applied Linguistics has evolved into a popular and effective way of designing lessons that effectively scaffold instruction for English learners' success. SIOP lessons include content-area objectives that are measureable and written in student-friendly language. Each lesson also includes a language objective that will receive focus throughout the instructional process. The language objectives relate to the content, and may relate to conventions, grammatical forms, reading skills and strategies, vocabulary, or writing. Materials necessary for scaffolding instruction are specifically identified, and the lesson design ensures that teachers prepare comprehensible input and that differential (including higher order) questions are pre-identified. Teachers specify how they will activate and build prior knowledge that links to students' past experiences and earlier learning, and they preview key vocabulary verbally and graphically. To further ensure that input is comprehensible, teacher talk and supports are targeted within and just beyond students' proficiencies and zones of proximal development. Planned interaction is appropriate to student readiness, the content and language objectives, and lesson tasks. Finally, teachers plan the specific ways in which they will assess lesson objectives. The gradual release of responsibility lesson design described in chapter 1 is a key feature of SIOP lessons, with the added attributes described here.

Thus far, this section has described practices related to the first task of English language instruction: English learners must successfully access content in multiple content areas for which instruction is typically provided in English. English language development must take place all day long, in every content area, and at every possible moment of the school day. Now let's turn to the second task of schools related to English learners: ensuring students develop native-like aptitudes in listening, speaking, reading, and writing across multiple content and discourse types.

Dedicated Content and Time of Day

There should be dedicated time during the instructional day (often thirty minutes) during which language objectives are primary in importance and content objectives are secondary. During this time for language development, language is in the foreground and whatever content teachers decide to embed this instruction in, whether English language arts, social studies, science, or some other content, is part of practice work and not the primary focus. The goal of this focused time is to apply the functions and grammatical forms of the English language in multiple content areas, orally and in writing, and in multiple settings.

This block of instruction is not for the rote memorization of English vocabulary. It is not filled with teachers talking and students passively listening. Rather, it includes systematically planned and explicitly executed instruction for which the focus is proficiently utilizing the English language. These lessons focus on the three Fs: function, form, and fluency (Dutro & Moran, 2003). Lessons are centered on distinct purposes (functions) of using the language. There are specific grammatical forms associated with functions. Teachers can differentiate the complexity of these forms based on students' English proficiency levels, and explicitly teach and repeatedly practice them in various ways applied to various contexts to develop high levels of fluency. The goals of units and lessons in English language development are to build on prior language and content knowledge; create authentic contexts for the purposeful, functional use of English; model comprehensible input and forms of language in a variety of meaningful ways; provide numerous opportunities for oral and written practice and application to develop fluency; and create positive, successful learning environments with immediate corrective feedback. Figure 4.1 (page 118) shows a sample unit of instruction for second-grade students at intermediate levels of proficiency. Additional samples appear in the appendix (pages 166–169).

Language function	Express needs and make requests
Grammar forms	Questions and statements with auxiliary verbs: *may, can, will*
Objective	We will use auxiliary verbs in order to express needs and make requests.
Topic	Classroom materials and procedures
Prompts and responses	Prompt: Can you please hand me the _____? Response: Can you please hand me the stapler? Prompt: Will you please give me the _____? Response: Will you please give me the stapler? Prompt: Here is the _____. Response: Here is the stapler. Prompt: Here are the _____. Response: Here are the staplers. Prompt: May I go to the _____? Response: May I go to the library? Prompt: Yes, you may go to the _____. Response: Yes, you may go to the library. Prompt: No, you may not go to the _____. Response: No, you may not go to the library.
Vocabulary	Book · Pen · Classroom
Application	Students will write a simple play with six exchanges between two friends who are asking one another for classroom materials.

Vocabulary columns:

Book	Pen	Classroom
Stapler	Marker	Cafeteria
Ruler	Social studies book	Bathroom
Paperclip	Science book	Library
Scotch tape	Math book	Gym
Masking tape	Glue	Office
Crayon	Paper	Playground
Dictionary	English book	
Journal	Textbook	
Notebook	Novel	

Figure 4.1: Sample second-grade English language development lesson.

The lesson lists the language function (or purpose) along with a grammatical form associated with this function—auxiliary verbs—and is based on the work of E. L. Achieve (2006). There is a suggested topic, but the language function could just as appropriately be embedded with English language arts, science, or social studies topics. In fact, the goal for students to apply the function and forms in any context. Topics should be those with which students have familiarity and experience; the cognitive load should primarily relate to the language function, not the topic or content. The lesson also includes possible vocabulary that students can practice using the sample prompts and responses. These prompts and responses are directly related to the function and forms. Finally, the lesson identifies a culminating unit activity that requires students to apply their language learning to another context. Units of instruction can span any number of days. Figure 4.2 (page 120) shows a general five-day unit of instruction.

During each of the approximately thirty minutes of daily English language development time, teachers should strive to ensure that students are engaged in oral or written expression for at least 50 percent of the lesson. During day one, the teacher activates and builds background knowledge and begins to introduce the vocabulary related to the chosen topic. On day two, the teacher reviews the topic vocabulary and students practice the first and more basic of the unit's prompts, responses, and language forms. On day three, students practice all prompts, responses, and forms. On day four, students practice all prompts and responses with partners and in unique contexts. Finally, on day five, students apply the prompts, responses, and forms that they have learned to unique contexts and to writing. These activities may be completed interactively with the teacher, in pairs, or independently based on each student's readiness. Throughout each lesson and throughout the five-day unit, teachers release responsibility to students at a rate that is appropriate for students' progress. The goal is not to teach English vocabulary; rather, the goal is for students to use grammatical forms for specific purposes or functions.

Instruction in English language development as a separate course can be organized along the major functions of languages: interpersonal communication, describing, classifying, comparing, and inferring. Teachers can perhaps select specific functions that match units of instruction in English language arts, science, and social studies. The sample units in the appendix (pages 166–169) provide guidance to teachers as they develop systematic units of explicit English language development.

Scaffolding for Success

Teachers should scaffold learning during both sheltered instruction and explicit English language development.

	Day One: Activate and Build Prior Knowledge and Introduce Topic Vocabulary	Day Two: Teach and Practice Basic Prompts and Responses	Day Three: Practice All Prompts and Responses	Day Four: Practice All Prompts and Responses With Partners in Unique Contexts	Day Five: Apply Prompts, Responses, and Forms to Unique Contexts and to Writing
Tasks	• Connect to prior knowledge or familiar content • Introduce vocabulary using maps and visual supports	• Introduce and practice the first prompts and responses • Practice with the entire class	• Introduce and practice the remaining prompts and responses • Practice with the entire class	• Practice all prompts and responses with partners and with new vocabulary	• Practice all prompts and responses with new vocabulary and in writing
Why Do It	We will listen and use statements and questions to contribute ideas to a discussion.	We will use new vocabulary and language patterns in order to communicate ideas.	We will use language patterns to communicate.	We will practice learned vocabulary and language patterns.	We will apply learned vocabulary and language patterns.
I Do It	• Read-aloud • Video • Songs, chants, poems • Visuals	• Thinking map • Pictorial input chart • Pantomime, gestures, chants • Echo/repeat response	• Sentence construction chart • Language patterns with stems • Language patterns with frames • Echo/repeat response		
We Do It Together		My turn/your turn	My turn/your turn	My turn/your turn	Interactive writing
You Do It Together		Talking sticks	Talking sticks	• Lines of communication • Tea party	
Closure	Think-pair-share Today I learned . . .	Think-pair-share Today I learned . . .	Think-pair-share Today I learned . . .	Think-pair-share Today I learned . . .	Think-pair-share Today I learned . . .

Figure 4.2: Sample five-day English language development unit of instruction.

Some strategies for scaffolding include the following:

- Graphic organizers
- Illustrated word banks
- Picture cards
- Realia
- Pantomimes
- Chants
- Language pattern charts
- Sentence stems
- Sentence frames
- Sentence construction charts

Structuring opportunities for students to practice using the English language are also critical. These fluency strategies include:

- Echo response
- Choral response
- My turn, your turn
- Language pattern songs
- Talking sticks
- Think-pair-share
- Think-write-share
- Structured role play

Teachers can differentiate instruction and construct language objectives in content areas or within the English language block of instruction by using WIDA's "Can Do" descriptors (WIDA, 2007). These descriptors define supports that can benefit students' receptive and expressive language, and they become increasingly complex as students progress from level 1 to level 5. Sample descriptors for grades 1 and 2 in reading and writing appear in Table 4.5 (page 122). These descriptors allow teachers to target and differentiate instruction while retaining the very highest of expectations for student mastery. They also help teachers interpret the meaning of a student's language proficiency level, as well as how a student should be able to perform in the classroom at each level.

Table 4.5: WIDA's Can Do Descriptors for Grades 1 and 2 Reading and Writing

Level 1	Level 2	Level 3	Level 4	Level 5
Reading				
• Identifies symbols, icons, and print • Connects print to visuals • Matches real-life objects to labels • Follows directions using diagrams or pictures	• Searches for pictures associated with word patterns • Identifies and interprets labeled diagrams • Matches voice to print by pointing to icons, letters, or illustrated words • Sorts words into families	• Makes text-to-self connections with prompting • Selects titles to match a series of pictures • Sorts illustrated words into categories • Matches phrases and sentences to pictures	• Puts words in order to form sentences • Identifies basic elements of fictional stories • Follows sentence-level directions • Distinguishes between general and specific language	• Uses features of nonfiction text to aid comprehension • Uses learning strategies • Identifies main ideas • Matches figurative language to illustrations
Writing				
• Copies written language • Uses first language to form words in English • Communicates through drawings • Labels familiar objects or pictures	• Provides information using graphic organizers • Generates words or phrases from banks • Completes modeled sentence starters • Describes people, places, or objects from illustrations and models	• Engages in prewriting strategies • Forms simple sentences using word banks • Participates in interactive journal writing • Gives content-based information using visuals	• Produces original sentences • Creates messages for social purposes • Composes journal entries about personal experiences • Uses classroom resources to compose sentences	• Creates a related series of sentences in response to prompts • Produces content-related sentences • Composes stories • Explains processes or procedures using connected sentences

Source: WIDA, 2007. Reprinted with permission.

Assessment of English Language Acquisition

In the United States, schools are required to administer annual tests to English learners that assess listening and speaking in kindergarten and listening, speaking, reading, and writing in first grade and above. An example of such a test is the Assessing Comprehension and Communication in English State to State (ACCESS) test produced by WIDA. The information these assessments provide is typically broad and not specific regarding student needs in their acquisition of English. However, educators can glean information that informs the supports schools provide. First, students are assigned proficiency levels based on their performance on these assessments. These levels then guide the appropriate grouping of students for instruction, as described in the previous section. In addition, educators can examine the listening, speaking, reading, and writing sub-goal data to identify individual or whole-group needs. Finally, comparing a student's proficiency level with his or her years in a U.S. school can help determine whether the student is progressing adequately in acquiring English. If a third grader who has attended U.S. schools since kindergarten is at a level 1 or beginning proficiency level, then the student is likely not acquiring English at an appropriate rate. While up to five to seven years may be required for English learners to fully develop academic proficiency with the English language (Cummins, 1986), a student whose English language proficiency has not markedly improved in three years should be of concern to educators. A student in this position would be a candidate for supplemental supports in addition to core English language development instruction.

Another excellent option to efficiently inform instructional decisions for English learners is a brief oral language probe, such as the Express Placement created by Susana Dutro and EL Achieve (Dutro, 2008). These probes, administered one on one, allow educators to listen to student's oral expression in minutes as students answer from six to twenty-four questions with increasingly difficult language demands. These probes provide educators with direct information on students' oral proficiency that allows for immediate adjustments to their instructional program.

English language screenings such as the ACCESS test are required to be given annually by federal and state law. Common formative assessments administered in between the annual required screenings are rarer. These assessments specifically assess students' development in the English language. Commercial programs may include these assessments, although they may not focus on the use (specifically oral and written expression) of English or on applications of the functions and forms of the language that should provide the focus for instruction. They may instead assess students' acquisition of vocabulary and not target students' use of English.

How might teachers begin to accomplish the task of frequently monitoring students' progress in English language development? They can start with creating or selecting appropriate common formative assessments. Teachers are becoming so much more adept and comfortable creating or selecting assessments that match and drive their instruction. These assessments are based on teachers' precise, agreed-upon identification of what students need to know, and they match the rigor and format of the standards. They provide evidence of learning in a common language that teachers can dialogue about and then use to inform instruction and interventions.

Building common assessments should be part of the instructional planning process in English language development. As teachers identify forms and language functions for an upcoming unit at students' selected proficiency levels, they can craft assessments that include tasks that are directly related to the application of the function and forms.

There is another manner in which teachers can monitor progress in the acquisition of English—one that allows teachers to use the information from existing assessments. Standards for the development of the English language from such organizations as TESOL and WIDA are, in part, designed to complement and support standards in English language arts. Therefore, it may be possible to use student progress on certain English language arts standards as a proxy for the development of English language. Moreover, there are certain standards that are more highly correlated to English language development than others. Thus, when teachers are developing and using common formative assignments in English language arts, they can specifically analyze whether English learners are successfully meeting and progressing in their mastery of these key English language arts standards. The possible key English language arts standards are listed in table 4.6.

Another potential tool is the Student Oral Language Observation Matrix (SOLOM) from the Center for Applied Linguistics (n.d.). The SOLOM is a set of structured tasks that can initially assess and then monitor the progress of English learners. Teachers use the SOLOM's rating scales to assess students' command of oral language based on listening comprehension, vocabulary, fluency, grammar, and pronunciation. However, the SOLOM assesses conversational proficiency and not the academic proficiency that educators need to ensure English learners develop. The SOLOM was not commercially published, but was developed by the San Jose Area Bilingual Consortium in partnership with the Bilingual Education Office of the California Department of Education. It is within the public domain and can be copied, modified, or adapted to meet local needs.

In addition, WIDA, through their partnership with school districts across the United States in the Formative Language Assessment Records for ELLs (FLARE) project, is developing and validating a formative assessment system for teachers serving English learners. Hopefully this project will provide insight and guidance for educators developing monitoring tools for English learners at all grade levels.

Table 4.6: English Language Arts Standards Related to English Language Acquisition

Kindergarten	First Grade	Second Grade	Third Grade
• Use nouns and verbs • Form regular plural nouns by adding /s/ or /es/ • Use question words • Use simple prepositions	• Use singular and plural nouns with matching verbs in basic sentences • Use personal, possessive, and indefinite pronouns • Use verbs to convey past, present, and future • Use conjunctions • Use determiners • Use prepositions • Produce complete simple and compound sentences	• Use collective nouns • Use irregular plural nouns • Use reflexive pronouns • Use the past tense of irregular verbs • Produce complete simple and compound sentences	• Use nouns, pronouns, verbs, adjectives, and adverbs • Use regular and irregular plural nouns • Use abstract nouns • Use simple verb tenses • Ensure subject-verb and pronoun-antecedent agreement • Use comparatives and superlatives • Produce simple, compound, and complex sentences

Source: TESOL, 2006.

English Language Interventions

Intervention as it relates to English learners is understandably complex and commonly confusing. Educators often wonder if English learners deemed at risk struggle as a result of language acquisition difficulties or from difficulties in reading, writing, or some other academic domain. While distinguishing between the two possible causes of difficulties is challenging, educators must not delay supporting English learners. Diagnosing the needs of English learners is no different than diagnosing the needs of any student: educators must meet with students one on one, analyze multiple forms of data, and collaboratively problem solve with members of their teacher team and other educators and specialists.

Educators should compare the English learner's years in school with his or her English proficiency level. When a student's English proficiency level is lower than that of his or her peers in the same grade level with the same number of years in school, then the student's struggles most likely are at least in part with English language acquisition. Educators can assess students' specific needs in English language development with assessments such as the Express Placement (Dutro, 2008) and by analyzing student strengths and needs relative to the Matrix of Grammatical Forms, both described in the previous section.

Teachers should be aware that students may struggle in content areas alongside their struggles with English. Teachers should assess and diagnose English learners in the same way for content area knowledge as they do for English-only students. When teachers know that students are still developing in their acquisition of English, whether at an appropriate or delayed rate, they must be prepared to assess student mastery of content in creative, differentiated ways, perhaps involving oral or visual means.

The Center on Instruction makes six recommendations for intervening with English learners (Rivera, Moughamian, Lesaux, & Francis, 2008). The first recommendation is to provide supports for English learners within an RTI model, such as the one articulated in this book and in Pyramid Response to Intervention (Buffum et al., 2009) and Simplifying Response to Intervention (Buffum et al., 2012). The second recommendation is to provide explicit, intensive intervention that is as specifically targeted to student needs as diagnoses allow. The next recommendation is to provide supports that address both early literacy skills, such as phonological awareness and phonics, and comprehension. Schools can provide these interventions through a single intervention program and within a single session or through multiple evidence-based intervention programs within multiple sessions. The fourth recommendation is to involve peers in supporting one another in developing reading skills. The fifth recommendation is an extra focus on building vocabulary and background knowledge when intervening with English learners. For English learners in particular, such an emphasis on vocabulary and background knowledge will also build word reading and word attack skills. The last recommendation is to equip English learners with tools that will allow them to read and make meaning of unfamiliar texts through independent and collaborative interactions with these texts.

While the Center for Instruction's six recommendations focus on reading, English learners may also have needs related to their acquisition of English. If students have English language acquisition needs, then schools must provide supplemental English language development time and support at the student's zone of proximal English language development. Using tools such as the Matrix of Grammatical Forms or assessments such as the Express Placement, teachers can determine if students' academic difficulties are impacted by their English language needs. Using tools such as those provided through the Consortium on Reading Excellence described in chapter 1, teachers can determine if students' academic difficulties are impacted by deficits in reading. Perhaps students will require differentiated and supplemental supports in both areas. The critically important point is that we do not assume that all English learners are deficient in reading, and yet we do not delay supports for English learners in reading simply because they are emerging at an entirely appropriate rate in their acquisition of the English language. English learners are students first; we must diagnose their precise needs to the greatest extent possible.

The Four Questions of RTI for English Learners

Teacher teams and schoolwide teams should regularly consider the following four questions when determining whether students are responding to instruction and intervention (Buffum et al., 2012):

1. **About which students do we have concerns?** Does your school systematically and carefully analyze results from the mandated state assessments given to all English learners and ensure that progress is adequate? Does your school supplement these standardized tests, whose results are not always delivered in a timely manner, with brief oral assessments, particularly when the English learner is at-risk in other areas.

2. **In what areas do we have concerns?** English learners are students first. English learners who are at risk do not necessarily have needs in the domain of English language acquisition. Ensure that all areas of schooling, including the student's English language skills, are diagnosed and examined when determining the most appropriate supports.

3. **What are we currently doing to support the student and meet the student's needs?** English learners are among the lowest performing students at many schools. Most school systems do not provide them with adequate supports. Provide explicit, Tier 1 English language development supports. Use effective strategies in all content areas to scaffold instruction: English language development should be the focus of instruction all day long. If, despite these core supports, English learners need supplemental supports in the area of English language, then this must be a priority.

4. **Has the student responded to the instruction and interventions (the supports) that we have been providing?** Until externally-produced progress monitoring assessments such as those under development by WIDA under the auspices of Project FLARE are widely available, schools must use teacher-created and teacher-selected common formative assessments and teacher evidence of student progress in relation to English language arts standards to monitor progress.

Summary

The statistics show that our schools are failing English learners. The work of Cummins (1986) and Krashen (1985) has long informed the types of supports and climates schools should provide for English learners, and their recommendations remain valid and appropriate; however, student performance data suggest that we must do more. Educators must consistently provide sheltered instruction throughout the school day to all English learners as well as systematic, explicit English language development supports, every day. English language development should be its own course and content area in which English learners practice using the English language for specific purposes. Teacher teams must define the essentials of English language development and design instructional units and employ instructional strategies that focus on language functions, grammatical forms, and fluency practice. When English learners receive core sheltered instruction and core English language development and their progress in acquiring English is still delayed, they must receive supplemental time and supports.

English learners are the lowest performing subgroup in so many American schools. This is not because these students are incapable of learning at the very highest levels. In fact, there are schools in which English learners are performing at levels equal to or above their English-only peers (Williams et al., 2007). To help English learners along the path to high achievement, educators must think and behave differently, beginning with respecting the incredible assets and background experiences that English learners bring to schools. Use the reproducible Guiding Goals for English Learners K–3 checklist to help determine the next steps you will take (in your classroom, team, school, or district) with your RTI-based English language development program.

The next chapter focuses on the critical role that partnerships between teachers and specialists can play in our schools. Teachers can proactively support students in grades K–3 as soon as they observe psychological, speech and language, behavioral, and fine-motor needs with the help of specialists. Teachers need not intervene intensively, but their early support in these areas can help prevent difficulties, disability-determinations, and perhaps most importantly, frustration and discouragement in students who then fall behind their peers.

Guiding Goals for English Learners K–3

Goal	Long-Term Vision	First Steps
Fully understand recent research and best practices in English language development	Staff collaboratively study recent research in English language development and blend these ideas with the existing research	☐ All staff engage in collaborative study of best practices in ensuring all students acquire English. ☐ Each teacher shares one key strategy for ensuring students successfully acquire English and access content.
Ensure that English learners receive explicit, systematic English language development	Staff provide English learners with at least thirty minutes a day of high-quality English language development as a dedicated course that focuses on the functions of language.	☐ Staff assess the needs of English learners and target instruction based on proficiencies and needs. ☐ Staff scope and sequence language functions, based on grade and proficiency, and match grammatical forms to the functions. ☐ Teacher teams collaboratively discover and share strategies to ensure that students build their fluency, speaking or writing at least 50 percent of class time.
Ensure that English learners, and all students, receive scaffolded supports within every content area	Staff develop and employ strategies so that language, vocabulary, and background knowledge are not limitations to the high levels of success of every student in every content area.	☐ Staff collaboratively explore and utilize strategies for organizing instruction (such as SIOP) and scaffolding content (such as SDAIE and Project GLAD). ☐ Teacher teams plan on regular (at least quarterly) lesson studies that focus on scaffolds, in which teachers co-plan, co-teach, and co-review lessons in one another's classroom.

CHAPTER 5

Students With Social/Emotional, Speech/Language, and Fine-Motor Challenges

*Education is a social process. Education is growth. Education
is not a preparation for life; education is life itself.*

JOHN DEWEY

As illustrated in previous chapters, waiting to intervene does not work. When our strategy is to wait for students to become developmentally ready and then allow them time to catch up, students are not successful; they are simply further behind. This applies not just to students in areas of reading, writing, and mathematics, but also to students with social/emotional, speech/language, and motor-skill challenges (Berninger et al., 1997; Berninger & Rutberg, 1992; Case-Smith, J., 2002; Catts, Fey, Tomblin, & Zhang, 2002; Dweck & Wortman, 1982; McIntosh, Chard, Boland, & Horner, 2006; Weintraub & Graham, 2000; Zins, Weissbert, Wang, & Walberg, 2004).

Students who are victims of such a wait-and-see approach to intervention have been impacted in other ways beyond the academic by the time they get to third grade. They have become frustrated and discouraged. Their attitudes and motivation have been affected. These students are doubly at risk—they are both academically and emotionally at risk. This chapter is about how educators must address students' social, behavioral, language, and motor-skill deficits early, and how they can do so with support from other school specialists. (Note that while the term *specialist* is used throughout this chapter, the focus is on clinicians. Special education teachers are most certainly specialists, but they have much more in common with general education classroom teachers than clinicians, since they share responsibilities and students with other teachers on school campuses.)

Key Content in the Social, Emotional, and Behavioral Domains

School psychologists should serve as key resources for classroom teachers as they ensure that students possess the social skills, behaviors, and cognitive functioning to succeed in school. The following skills are those with which school psychologists can assist students and staff. The purpose of defining such skills is twofold: (1) so that teachers and other school personnel can be on the lookout for students who may exhibit these challenges, and (2) to develop supports and strategies to remediate before deficits become extreme.

- **Social skills:** The set of skills people use to interact and communicate with one another, including turn-taking in conversation, maintaining conversation, and eye contact

- **Behaviors:** Personal characteristics and attributes, including externalizing behaviors (stealing, lying, cheating, sneaking, negative attitude, or aggressive behavior) and internalizing behaviors (nervousness, fearfulness, spending time alone, withdrawing, sadness, or complaining about being sick or hurt)

- **Attention deficits:** Attributes of such deficits include inadequate attention to details, consistent careless mistakes, lack of focus during play, appearing not to listen, daydreaming, failing to follow instructions, failing to finish tasks, avoiding tasks that require mental endurance or organization, frequently losing items required for tasks, distractibility, forgetfulness, and procrastination

- **Self-regulatory strategies:** The process of activating and sustaining internal, self-control behaviors to systematically attain goals

  + *Metacognition*—Knowledge and beliefs about thinking

  + *Self-concept*—Seeing oneself as smart

  + *Self-monitoring*—The ability to plan and prepare

  + *Motivation*—The ability to maintain interest

  + *Strategy*—Techniques for organization and memorization

  + *Volition*—The efforts needed to stay motivated

- **Cognitive functioning:** The process of accessing, storing, connecting, retrieving, and applying knowledge

  + *Short-term memory*—Temporarily storing and managing information required to carry out complex cognitive tasks, including encoding, storing, and retrieving data

  + *Long-term memory*—The ability to recall sensations, events, ideas, and other information for long periods of time, usually divided into declarative memory (episodic memory of specific events and semantic memory about the world) and procedural memory (memories of body movement and how to use objects in one's environment)

  + *Visual processing*—The ability to make sense of information taken in through the eyes, affecting how visual information is interpreted by the brain, and including

    - Spatial relation. The position of objects in space and the ability to accurately perceive objects in space with reference to other objects

    - Visual discrimination. The ability to differentiate objects (color, form, shape, pattern, size, and position) based on individual characteristics, and the ability to recognize an object as distinct from its surroundings

    - Visual closure. The ability to identify or recognize a symbol or object when the entire object is not visible

    - Object recognition. The ability to recognize familiar objects or objects recognizable through other senses; the ability to integrate various visual stimuli into a recognizable whole; the ability to retrieve the mental representation of an object; and the ability to connect the mental representation to the object

    - Whole/part relationships. The ability to perceive or integrate the relationship between an object and its parts

  + *Auditory processing*—The ability to make sense of information taken in through the ears, affecting how auditory information is interpreted by the brain (may also be under the domain of speech and language and may affect reading and writing), including

    - Phonological awareness. The understanding that language is made up of individual sounds that are put together to form the words we write and speak, and the ability to recognize or isolate the individual sounds in a word, recognize similarities between words (rhyming), or be able to identify the number of sounds in a word

- Auditory discrimination. The ability to recognize differences in sounds

- Auditory memory. The ability to store and recall information given verbally

- Auditory sequencing. The ability to remember or reconstruct the order of items in a list or the order of sounds in a word or syllable

- Auditory blending. The process of putting sounds together to form words

+ *Reasoning skills*—Processes basic to all forms of cognition

  - Storage and retrieval skills. The ability to transfer information to and from long-term memory and relate new data to information already in long-term memory

  - Matching skills. The ability to determine how incoming information is similar to or different from information already stored in long-term memory

    * Categorization: The ability to classify objects or ideas as belonging to a group and having the characteristics of that group, also known as *chunking*

    * Extrapolation: The ability to match the pattern of information from one area to that found in another area, to avoid starting from scratch when encountering new information

    * Analogical reasoning: The ability to see similarities among objects or ideas and the use of existing knowledge to understand new information

    * Evaluation of logic: Determining whether the structure of information with a system of logic is valid or true

    * Evaluation of value: The process of determining whether information is relevant

  - Executive procedures. Processes that coordinate other skills so that new cognitive structures can be built

    * Elaboration: The process of inferring information using storage, retrieval, and matching skills when the learning situation is incomplete

    * Problem solving: The process of finding information or a strategy to achieve a goal

    * Composing: The process of creating new information to express an idea, usually orally or in writing

If teachers and other staff members are aware of these skills that are within psychologists' sphere of knowledge, they can communicate to school leadership teams when there is a need for the psychologist's support, and educators can observe, screen, and provide the necessary preventative supports to ensure students do not fall behind or become frustrated.

Instruction and Intervention in the Social, Emotional, and Behavioral Domains

When teams determine that students in early elementary grades may be exhibiting consistent difficulties with the skills listed in the previous section, psychologists and school administrators should assist in diagnosing specific needs and provide teachers with the knowledge, skills, and strategies necessary to provide in-class supports to students. The following are a sampling of researched-based supports:

- Social skills
    + Assign peer buddies or assign students to peer groups.
- Behaviors
    + Analyze the function (purpose) of misbehavior.
    + Teach and model desired behavior.
    + Identify positive reinforcers.
    + Implement behavior contracts.
- Attention
    + Develop signals to refocus a student.
    + Employ predictable structures, routines, and procedures.
    + Reinforce auditory directions with pictures and other visual supports.
    + Be prepared to try new approaches with specific students that are different than those used for the rest of the class.
    + Chunk assignments, even assigning one task at a time.
    + Gain students' attention, call individuals by name, and establish eye contact before providing the directions.
    + When finished giving directions to the entire class, restate the directions to students who appear to need assistance, and have them repeat the directions back as a check for understanding.
    + Randomly call on students, occasionally selecting the same student twice in a row or within a short time span.

+ During whole-group activities, circulate around the room and stand or sit near the student in need before giving directions or engaging in discussion.

+ Give clear directions at a pace that does not overwhelm the student in need, post directions for later review, or give directions to students as a handout.

+ Allow students a list of assignment choices with which teachers are comfortable.

+ Instruct at a brisk pace, ensuring that lessons are fully prepared and minimizing housekeeping and transitions.

+ Whenever and however possible, make connections to students' real-world situations, and plan for frequent, structured interactions with peers.

+ Make an effort to identify times when an off-task student is appropriately focused on the lesson and give immediate positive reinforcement.

+ Provide a quiet work area, such as a desk or study carrel, but never use the area as a punitive time-out space.

+ Establish behavior contracts with students that allow them short breaks for a preferred activity after they have finished a defined amount of work.

+ Trim assignments to the minimum length necessary to ensure student understanding, and when practicing or reviewing skills previously taught, break tasks into a series of short assignments.

+ Schedule challenging tasks early in the day; save easier subjects or tasks for later in the day.

+ Avoid long stretches of instructional time in which students sit passively.

+ Schedule instructional activities so that students must frequently and actively show what they know.

+ Train students to transition appropriately by demonstrating how they should prepare for common activities, such as group work and independent seatwork, and alert students several minutes prior to a transition to another activity.

+ Provide students with a visible, tangible schedule of the lesson's or day's activities.

+ Seat students who are at risk within the zone in which most attention is focused.

- Self-regulatory strategies

    + Show students how to cope with worry.

    + Show students how to self-test to check for understanding.

+ Show students how to prepare for class.

+ Show students how to develop self-discipline.

+ Show students how to organize supplies.

+ Show students how to organize knowledge.

+ Show students how to identify the most important information to learn.

+ Show students how to reason through to an answer.

+ Show students how to create and follow a schedule.

+ Show students how to deal with distractions, competing goals, and procrastination.

+ Show students how to better concentrate.

+ Show students how to prioritize.

The most systematic, practical, and successful way of ensuring that students behave, are attentive, and are engaged in learning is to build a schoolwide system of positive behavioral supports. While the collective commitment required to build schoolwide supports is high, the steps are simple and the benefits to students and learning environments are enormous (Buffum et al., 2012; Hierck et al., 2011). First, schools must explicitly define desired student behaviors and commit to consistently teaching and reinforcing these behaviors. This includes both social and academic behaviors. Next, educators explicitly teach these desired behaviors to every student and explain them to every stakeholder. To determine students who may be immediately in need of extra support, the school screens for behavioral challenges and identifies what types of supports are necessary and the staff members who can provide them. This is followed by creating a system for monitoring behavior and identifying positive reinforcers, consequences, and supports for students who are at risk.

There are also strategies for addressing student needs in cognitive areas, such as the following:

- Address short-term memory challenges by
    + Breaking instruction into smaller chunks
    + Assigning repeated practice immediately upon learning new information that is closely related in format and rigor to the ways in which the information was initially taught; asking students to apply new learning to new situations, but not too quickly
    + Providing visual cues and prompts
- Address long-term memory challenges by
    + Assigning tasks that apply new learning

- + Using KWL-like charts and KWL-inspired tasks that activate background knowledge so that students are more likely to build on prior knowledge

- Address visual-processing challenges by
  - + Providing more auditory instruction, and combining visual with auditory instruction
  - + Providing large-print books, papers, worksheets, and other materials
  - + Creating "windows" by cutting a rectangle in an index card to help keep relevant numbers, words, and sentences in clear focus while blocking out peripheral material
  - + Providing rulers to keep relevant information in focus
  - + Making lines on paper darker and more distinct for writing tasks
  - + Providing paper with raised lines to provide kinesthetic feedback
  - + Reducing the amount of content on each page of an activity

- Address auditory-processing challenges by
  - + Providing more visual instruction, and combining auditory with visual instruction
  - + Slowing the rate of speech and minimizing distractions when giving verbal directions
  - + Playing rhyming games and attempting to embed rhymes in directions and instruction
  - + Providing written steps for all types of problem-solving situations, not just those for which steps may be typical

- Address reasoning challenges by providing explicit and consistent practice and support in organizing, synthesizing, drawing conclusions, making connections, and inferring

If we delay implementing simple and effective strategies such as those just listed while we wait for newer, better strategies, we will remain frustrated and continue to underserve and undersupport students. The success of a strategy has far more to do with consistent, appropriate application than on its research base. A more professional and successful approach is to collaboratively identify a set of simple strategies, implement them with care and a sense of urgency, and collaboratively monitor, analyze, and revise their use based on assessments.

Assessment in the Social, Emotional, and Behavioral Domains

Psychologists can also be of great assistance in preliminarily assessing and observing students in order to provide guidance to teachers on the most appropriate supports for students who are at risk. Psychologists may gather anecdotal records after observing a student in multiple school settings and may use this information to complete the following assessments:

- Behavioral Observation of Students in Schools (BOSS)

- Behavior Assessment System for Children (BASC-2)

- Student Risk Screening Scale (SRSS) or Student Internalizing Behavior Screening Scale (SIBSS)

- A simplified functional behavior analysis or antecedents-behavior-consequences chart, available at **www.solution-tree.com/rti**

- A self-regulatory assessment and problem-solving tool, available at **www.solution -tree.com/rti**

When monitoring the progress of students in these areas, data from check-in/check-out (CICO) procedures, such as the sample provided in the appendix on page 170, can help teams determine if students are responding to supports.

These assessments are very helpful, though the most important ways in which psychologists can assess student needs are likely much more informal. Observing a student in various settings (with appropriate permissions) or engaging in collaborative dialogues about students will likely yield insights and produce ideas for interventions that will help students be more successful.

Key Content in Speech and Language

Virtually every primary teacher has known a student with speech articulation challenges— perhaps the challenges were not enough that the student was technically developmentally delayed, but the difficulties did complicate the student's ability to coherently manipulate phonemes. Speech and language supports ensure students can clearly articulate their learning orally and that they possess the language to succeed. Speech and language pathologists can assist students with the following:

- **Articulation challenges**—Errors in speech sounds that interfere with intelligibility, including the omission, distortion, substitution, addition, or incorrect sequencing of sounds

- **Phonological and auditory processing challenges**—Errors resulting from impairments in the organization of phonemes; producing a sound correctly but not using it appropriately, displaying a reduced sound inventory, or hearing sounds but not processing them correctly into words

- **Syntax challenges**—Errors in constructing grammatically correct sentences and phrases

- **Semantic challenges**—Errors in knowledge of word meaning or in knowing the difference between literal and figurative language

- **Pragmatic challenges**—Errors in the use of language and behaviors in social contexts, with specific difficulties in:

  + What to say

  + How to say it

  + When to say it

  + How to behave with other people

  + How to use language socially in ways typical of age-alike children

  + How to take turns in conversations

  + How to respond with appropriate pauses or silences

  + Appropriate volumes of voice to use when responding

  + When to, and when not to, interrupt

  + Which topics listeners may, and may not, have interest in

  + When to assume and when not to assume prior knowledge

  + How much prior knowledge to assume

  + How much detail to include in stories

  + How long to tell stories

Younger children are likely to display many of these characteristics at various times. When a student exhibits deficiencies in these areas that are distinct from the patterns of his or her peers, or when these behaviors interfere with the student's success, speech and language pathologists can assist in specifically assessing needs and suggesting targeted supports.

Instruction and Intervention in Speech and Language

Intervening or providing preventative supports in speech and language often involves providing systematic, explicit instruction in areas that other students seem to have learned automatically.

The following activities could be completed in small groups within core, Tier 1 differentiated supports:

- Articulation
    + Playing games to practice *r*, *s*, *l*, *sh*, and *ch* sounds
    + Playing games that include tongue twisters and Mad Lib activities
- Phonological and auditory processing
    + Rhyming
    + Listening for initial, medial, or final sounds
    + Matching words to pictures
    + Counting syllables
    + Producing consonant digraphs
    + Differentiating among auditory signals, speech patterns, and pitch changes
    + Conceptualizing auditory messages to give meaning to auditory inputs by providing or activating background knowledge to ensure that deficits in processing are not the result of a lack of understanding of the concept itself
    + Successfully anticipating sounds by synthesizing the context of the situation
- Syntax
    + Practicing subject-verb agreement
    + Writing descriptions of adjectives
    + Sorting words based on common attributes
    + Defining nouns using visual aids
    + Practicing irregular plurals, possessives, or pronouns
    + Responding to what, where, when, why, and who questions
- Semantics
    + Naming common objects and using positional words
    + Providing or following directions, sequences, and procedures
    + Applying analogies, prefixes, suffixes, multiple meanings, and prepositions
    + Using homonyms, homophones, synonyms, and antonyms
    + Determining the meaning of idioms and figurative language
- Pragmatics
    + Practicing the facial expressions for various emotions

+ Practicing how to answer basic social questions, such as, "How are you doing?"

+ Practicing appropriate voice levels in various settings

+ Practicing identifying emotions by selecting the correct picture

+ Practicing when to take turns with another speaker

+ Practicing how to respond to nonverbal cues, such as body language and mood

+ Practicing when and how to introduce a new topic into a conversation

+ Practicing when to maintain a topic, when to change the topic, and how to interrupt appropriately

+ Practicing when to maintain eye contact and when to look away

+ Practicing how to talk and behave in formal and informal situations

+ Practicing how to expand thoughts and give brief responses

+ Practicing allowing for appropriate personal space

+ Practicing using appropriate words and behaviors regarding being polite in social, playground, and classroom situations

+ Practicing managing frustration, anger, and conflict

Interventions and supports that address speech and language deficits need not be complicated, and they don't have to be administered by a specialist. Teachers can embed them into their classroom instruction and track student improvement from week to week.

Assessment in Speech and Language

Speech and language pathologists can be of great assistance in assessing and observing students in order to provide guidance to teachers on the most appropriate supports. In the areas of articulation, phonological and auditory processing, syntax, semantics, and pragmatics, speech and language pathologists may gather anecdotal records after observing a student in multiple school settings (with appropriate permissions). They may use any of the following forms of assessment or data-collection tools:

- Checklists, observations, and interviews allow educators to gather information from multiple perspectives and environments. They are easy to administer and can be adapted to grade-level content.

- Criterion-referenced measures, development scales, and play-based assessments are designed to be used in natural settings, can be used to document progress over time, and are helpful in developing intervention plans.

- Dynamic assessments distinguish speech and language impairments from English language differences.

- Language sampling and speech intelligibility tests measure communication skills during educational settings through approaches such as Systematic Analysis of Language Transcripts (SALT) and Developmental Sentence Scoring (DSS).

Some types of assessment may be more appropriate to use in early, preventative efforts. Shared knowledge of the domain of speech and language helps facilitate discussions about student needs between teachers and specialists so that students receive the appropriate supports.

Key Content in Fine-Motor Skills

One of the most significant impacts of fine-motor-skill challenges is on students' writing ability. When students lack confidence and competence in their fine-motor abilities, their writing may be negatively impacted, so students are at a disadvantage when trying to express their understanding. Students for whom writing is difficult and who do not experience success in writing may not be motivated to write as often as their peers. While the potentially negative impacts of fine-motor difficulties on writing are perhaps most obvious and profound, difficulties may also impact performance in art (cutting with scissors), play (hand-eye coordination), and reading (turning pages) in less direct ways, but in ways that are still frustrating to students and may interact with or exacerbate other challenges. When teachers have concerns about students' fine-motor skills, visual-perceptual skills, and sensory-processing skills, they can consult occupational therapists to provide assistance with diagnoses and potential supports. Occupational therapists can help students improve the following skills:

- Fine-motor
    + Moving the hands, wrists, and arms, including dexterity, coordination, and strength
    + Dressing and grooming
    + Manipulating objects such as puzzles, books, scissors, and pencils
    + Copying shapes, letters, numbers, and designs
    + Handwriting
- Visual-perceptual
    + Using visual motor abilities and hand-eye coordination
    + Correctly spacing words when writing
    + Organizing a locker or desk
    + Hitting a target, batting a ball, or copying from a blackboard

- Sensory-processing
    + Receiving, organizing, and interpreting physical input
    + Planning for motor use
    + Reading physical cues when practicing behavior and social skills
    + Listening and following directions that require movement

Instruction and Intervention in Fine-Motor Skills

Teachers, in consultation with occupational therapists, may work with students in small groups or individually when it is determined that students would benefit from support in motor skills. Improving fine-motor, visual-perceptual, and sensory-processing skills may involve:

- Tracing, tracking, and copying to improve hand-eye coordination
- Conceptualizing what each body part needs to do in order to complete a task
- Knowing how much physical pressure is needed to complete a task
- Improving in-hand manipulation
- Improving arm, hand, and finger strength and stability
- Practicing finger succession, lifting, spreading, localization, and recognition
- Increasing tripod grip strength

Assessment in Fine-Motor Skills

Students in need of motor-skill supports or interventions may have the following symptoms:

- Trembling or weak hands
- Difficulty writing, drawing, or cutting
- Difficulty learning to ride a bike, hop on one foot, skip, climb, run, perform jumping jacks, hit a ball, roller skate, and so on
- Difficulty dressing or brushing teeth
- Over- or under-sensitivity to tactile or sensory input
- Walking too hard, pushing too hard, writing too hard, playing with objects too hard, and so on
- Behaving too loudly or roughly, crashing, shaking, jumping, and bouncing
- Shaking legs or constantly tapping feet

- Cracking knuckles, chewing fingers, biting nails, as well as chewing on pens, gum, pencils, clothing, strings, or objects

- Difficulty tying shoes

- Frequently bumping into objects and people accidentally

- Tripping and falling often

- Experiencing fear or difficulty going up and down stairs or escalators

- Slumping at desk, dinner table, and so on

- Consistently appearing to be limp and lethargic

- Needing to rest head on hands or lay head down while working

- Exhibiting poor posture during motor tasks

- Exhibiting inability to stand on one foot and difficulty with balancing tasks

An occupational therapy evaluation assesses:

- **Gross motor skills**—Movement of the large muscles in the arms and legs

- **Fine-motor skills**—Movement and dexterity of the small muscles in the hands and fingers

- **Visual motoring skills**—Movement based on the perception of visual information

- **Handwriting skills**—Coordination of eyes, arms, hands, pencil grip, letter formation, and body posture

- **Daily living skills**—Daily dressing, feeding, and toilet tasks

- **Oral motor skills**—Movement of muscles in the mouth, lips, tongue, and jaw, including sucking, biting, chewing, and licking

- **Motor planning skills**—Ability to plan, implement, and sequence motor tasks

- **Sensory integration skills**—Ability to take in, sort out, and respond to the input received from the world

- **Sensory processing skills**—Ability to take in sensory (vision, auditory, olfactory, tactile, tasting, vestibular [movement information/balance]), and proprioceptive (where your body is in space) information and organize the information to make sense

If teachers observe students who exhibit many of these deficiencies with consistency, it should prompt a conversation among teachers, administrators, and specialists. The goal is to proactively provide supports within the regular classroom as part of core, Tier 1 instruction, and to provide additional early intervention if Tier 1 supports prove insufficient.

The Four Questions of RTI for Students With Social/Emotional, Speech/Language, and Fine-Motor Challenges

Teacher teams and schoolwide teams should regularly consider the following four questions when determining whether students are responding to instruction and intervention (Buffum et al., 2012):

1. **About which students do we have concerns?** Teams should spend time identifying and understanding the skills psychologists, speech and language pathologists, and occupational therapists bring to schools. This may involve scheduling time for these specialists to train classroom teachers about signs of concern in students. Additionally, specialists should train classroom teachers on strategies they can use within the classroom to provide preliminary preventative supports.

2. **In what areas do we have concerns?** The training that specialists facilitate should provide simple and valid observation tools that allow teams of teachers to identify an at-risk student's specific area of need.

3. **What are we currently doing to support the student and meet the student's needs?** The systems that regularly identify students about whom teachers may have concerns should also address who will provide supports, when, how, and with what strategies, materials, or resources.

4. **Has the student responded to the instruction and interventions (the supports) that we have been providing?** When teams have identified student needs, teachers are in a position to monitor the progress that students are making. It need not be complicated; teams must simply commit to regularly (every week or two weeks) recording their observations of students in specific areas and compare these observations to prior observations.

Summary

Students with social, behavioral, speech, language, and motor-skill deficits in the early grades often fall behind, become frustrated, or both. They don't simply fall behind in these specific domains; these deficits can lead to difficulties in other areas. The solution need not be more students receiving special education services; the initial solution may simply be building shared knowledge between specialists and classroom teachers regarding basic ways in which students can improve these skills within core instruction. Use the reproducible Guiding Goals for K–3 Emotional/Behavioral, Speech/Language, and Motor-Skill Challenges checklist to help determine the next steps you will take (in your classroom, team, school, or district) in your RTI-based work with students.

Guiding Goals for K–3 Emotional/Behavioral, Speech/Language, and Fine-Motor Challenges

Goal	Long-Term Vision	First Steps
Facilitate frequent dialogue between specialists and classroom teachers	Specialists and classroom teachers meet weekly to build shared knowledge on the skills represented within the specialists' domains and to problem solve regarding students in need.	☐ Teacher teams invite specialists to participate in all school functions. ☐ The school provides opportunities for specialists to teach all other staff members about the skills represented within the specialists' domains.
Create a focus on the social-emotional-behavioral development of students	Staff, with guidance from school psychologists, counselors, and social workers, monitor a system of positive schoolwide expectations and supports.	☐ All staff build shared knowledge around the content and resources in the areas of behavior and social development. ☐ The school establishes a core, Tier 1 system of consistent behavioral expectations and supports.
Frequent screening and early intervention	Student needs in the domains represented by specialists (social/emotional, speech/language, motor skills) are regularly screened, and immediate, early supports are provided when needs are identified.	☐ Identify when, and with what tools, the domains of specialists (social/emotional, speech/language, motor skills) will be screened. ☐ Build early intervention in these skills into the routine of daily instruction.

EPILOGUE

*Effective schools get that way partly by making it
clear that pupil acquisition of basic school skills takes
precedence over all other school activities.*

RON EDMONDS

In the late 1970s, Ron Edmonds and the other founders of the Effective Schools movement understood the challenges schools face and envisioned the solutions with clarity. To paraphrase Edmonds from one seminal article: we already know everything we need to help all students achieve success (Edmonds, 1979). Today, we can envision and describe—with more clarity than ever before—schools that will prepare all students for college or a skilled career. RTI represents the best framework on which to build this reality (Buffum et al., 2012).

There have been two recurrent themes in this book. First, without well-developed literacy and numeracy skills by the end of third grade and at each grade level along the way, students will very likely experience difficulties in fourth grade and beyond, difficulties that will require remedial supports. These supports will likely, and necessarily, be provided at the expense of elective opportunities (such as art, music, and technology) or even at the expense of core content (such as science and social studies) that develop the skills students require to be ready for college or a skilled career. Second, when students are assessed to be falling behind in their development of high levels of literacy and numeracy in kindergarten, first grade, second grade, and third grade, intervention should occur immediately and with intensity—even in the earliest grades. The skills students should master also include social, behavioral, language, and motor skills.

Often the curricula and instructional strategies that are touted as most appropriate for primary-grade students have represented a singular point of view. Whether in reading, writing, mathematics, or English language development, common approaches to instruction have been incomplete. In reading, phonics and whole language have competed for teacher support, though both are necessary. In writing, writer's workshop and structured writing have loyal followers and believers;

however, they are compatible. In mathematics, conceptually dominant or procedurally dominant programs have been implemented separately, but they are mutually reinforcing. In English language development, natural and explicit approaches have been at odds, though they both serve a critical role.

The ways in which educators have traditionally viewed instruction in kindergarten through third grade, while well intended and successful for some, have been incomplete. Educators have the skills, expertise, and experiences required to ensure that every kindergartener, first grader, second grader, and third grader is learning at the very highest levels. When we truly and unanimously accept the goal of high levels of learning for every student within every grade level as the responsibility of every staff member, and when we demonstrate a willingness to do whatever it takes to make that happen, we cannot fail. If we compromise expectations for students or ourselves or bicker based on ideological points of view, we will not succeed. In order to close the knowing-doing gap, we must understand the following points:

- Fourth grade is too late to begin intervening; we must leverage our resources and personnel and make a commitment to intervene early.

- More-intensive supports provided for brief periods of time are superior to less-intensive supports over months and years; we must commit to intervening with a sense of urgency.

- A guaranteed and viable curriculum in both academic and behavioral domains is a moral and practical imperative; we must exercise courage to expect all staff to participate in collaborative practices and focus our curriculum.

- Fluency and vocabulary have been under-represented curricularly and instructionally; we must fill these gaps in our core curriculum and remediate with students we have failed.

- Collaboration among educators is one of the most research-validated practices at our disposal. We must set norms and expectations for collaboration. Autonomy is not an attribute of professionalism in education.

- Behavior and academics are linked; we must explicitly teach them both, expect the most of students in both, and diagnose needs in both.

- Oral and written expression pose challenges that can impede students' ability to produce work that demonstrates their mastery; we must be prepared to provide stems, frames, and structures to scaffold students to word success.

- English learners' acquisition of skills often stalls at the intermediate range when supports end prematurely; we must modify time and support for students in need, embed supports in all content areas, and extend supports for longer periods of time.

- Fluency in math facts specifically, and number sense more generally, are keys to successfully engaging in critical thinking, problem solving, and more complex mathematics; we must intensively and explicitly teach these skills in kindergarten through third grade.

- Students who master consonant-vowel-consonant phonics with some degree of difficulty may later experience difficulty with multisyllabic phonics; we must provide instruction in advanced phonics for all students and be prepared to intervene in the area of phonics in the upper grades.

As a framework for school improvement, RTI provides educators with a golden opportunity. It helps ensure that all students learn at high levels when they receive core instruction and intervention. Yet educators frequently miss this golden opportunity when they focus RTI implementation and intervention on students in grades 4 and above in an effort to respond to students whose challenges have been over four years in the making. We must continue to support such students, but we must also proactively support students in kindergarten through third grade so that they are on track from the beginning. The goal is not just intervention—it's prevention. Our actions must match the commonly held belief that early, intensive interventions will prevent future educational emergencies.

APPENDIX

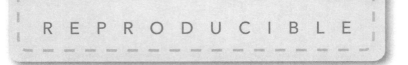

Reading Domains, Skills, and Assessments

This table can help teams identify where in the literacy continuum a student's reading is breaking down. By starting from the top left and working down and then to the right, teams may be able to determine where to begin intervening with a student.

CORE assessments can be found at: www.corelearn.com

DIBELS assessments can be found at: dibels.uoregon.edu

QRI (*Qualitative Reading Inventory*, 5th edition) can be found at: www.pearsonhighered.com

easyCBM assessments can be found at: http://easycbm.com

	Phonemic Awareness (Phonological Awareness)	Phonics	Fluency	Vocabulary	Comprehension
Assessment Types Universal screening Progress monitoring Diagnostic	DIBELS Next (FSF & PSF) easyCBM CORE	DIBELS Next (LNF & NWF) CORE	DIBELS Next (ORF) CORE easyCBM	DIBELS Next (Daze) CORE	DIBELS Next (Daze) CORE QRI easyCBM
Skills Within Reading Domains Skills are developed from left to right and top to bottom.	Listen for sounds	Letter–sound correspondence	Accuracy	Word classification	Vocabulary
	Rhyming words	High-frequency words	Rate	Antonyms and synonyms	Concept development
	Initial sounds	Short vowels	Prosody	Affixes and roots	Background knowledge
	Words in sentences	Consonant blends		Multiple-meaning words	Academic language
	Syllables in words	Long vowels		Homophones and homographs	Genre

page 1 of 2

Skills Within Reading Domains Skills are developed from left to right and top to bottom.	Track and order phonemes	Vowel digraphs and diphthongs		Word learning strategies	Text structure
	Phoneme isolation	R-controlled		Word origins and derivatives	Comprehension skills
	Phoneme identification	Multisyllabic words		Figurative language and idioms	Comprehension strategies
	Phoneme comparison	Compound words			
	Phoneme blending	Contractions			
	Phoneme segmentation	Inflectional forms			
	Phoneme deletion				
	Phoneme addition				
	Phoneme substitution				

FSF = first sound fluency; PSF = phoneme segmentation fluency; LNF = letter naming fluency; NWF = nonsense word fluency; ORF = oral reading fluency.

RTI in the Early Grades © 2013 Solution Tree Press • solution-tree.com
Visit **go.solution-tree.com/rti** to download this page.

Kindergarten Monitoring Tool

Skills	Teacher Notes	
Concepts of Print		
Identifies the front cover of a book		
Identifies the back cover of a book		
Identifies the title page of a book		
Follows words from left to right		
Follows words from top to bottom		
Follows words from page to page		
Recognizes that spoken words are represented by specific sequences of letters		
Understands that words are separated by spaces		
Phonological Awareness and Phonemic Awareness		
Recognizes rhyming words: "Say *ham, rod, jam.* Which two words rhyme?"		
Produces rhyming words: "What word rhymes with . . ." (*pig, fun, ball*)		
Counts and segments syllables in spoken words: "Clap the syllables in . . ."		
Blends syllables in spoken words		
Blends onsets and rimes of single-syllable spoken words		
Segments onsets and rimes of single-syllable spoken words		
Segments the initial, medial-vowel, and final sounds in consonant-vowel-consonant words (not /l/, /r/, or /x/ endings)		
Adds sounds to one-syllable words to make new words		
Substitutes sounds in one-syllable words to make new words		
Phonics and Fluency		
Names all uppercase and lowercase letters		
Produces the sounds for each consonant		

RTI in the Early Grades © 2013 Solution Tree Press • solution-tree.com
Visit **go.solution-tree.com/rti** to download this page.

Produces the long and short sounds for each vowel	
Reads common high-frequency words	
Distinguishes between similarly spelled words by identifying the sounds of letters that differ	
Comprehension and Vocabulary	
Asks and answers questions about key details	
Identifies the main topic and retells key details	
Identifies the reasons an author gives to support points	
Identifies characters	
Identifies settings	
Identifies major events	
Asks and answers questions about unknown words	
Recognizes types of texts (such as storybooks and poems)	
Names the author and illustrator and defines their roles	
Describes the relationship between illustrations and the story	
Compares and contrasts: • Experiences of characters in familiar stories • Illustrations, descriptions, or procedures • Two individuals, events, ideas, or pieces of information	
Actively engages in group reading activities	

RTI in the Early Grades © 2013 Solution Tree Press • solution-tree.com
Visit **go.solution-tree.com/rti** to download this page.

First-Grade Monitoring Tool

Skills	Teacher Notes	
Concepts of Print		
Recognizes the distinguishing features of a sentence (Present student with a book, and ask, "Show me a capital letter. Show me a word. Show me a sentence. Show me a period.")		
Phonological Awareness (Includes Phonemic Awareness)		
Distinguishes long from short vowel sounds in spoken single-syllable words (Use words with long- and short-vowel sounds to prompt a student to distinguish between long- and short-vowels in words: "Which word has a long-vowel sound? Short-vowel sound?")		
Produces single-syllable words by blending sounds, including consonant blends (Give student two to four individual phonemes. Student blends phonemes to make word: "What word do I have if I put together the sounds . . ." Example phonemes include /k/a/n/, /f/l/a/t/, /i/t/, /sh/ir/t/, /c/a/t/ = cat /f/l/a/t/ = flat.)		
Isolates initial, medial vowel, and final sounds in single-syllable words (Prompt student to identify initial, medial, and final sounds in single-syllable words: "What is the initial sound in . . . ; what is the medial or middle sound in . . . ; what is the final or ending sound in . . ." Example words include *seat*, *patch*, *cart*, *chip*.)		
Segments single-syllable words into their sequence of individual sounds (Use single-syllable words to prompt a student to segment words into their components: "What are the sounds in . . . ?" Example single-syllable words include *splat*, *rich*, *trap*, *duck*—cat = /c/a/t/; splat = /s/p/l/a/t/; rich = /r/i/ch/; trap = /t/r/a/p/; duck = /d/u/c/k/)		

RTI in the Early Grades © 2013 Solution Tree Press • solution-tree.com

Visit **go.solution-tree.com/rti** to download this page.

Phonics and Fluency	
Knows the spelling-sound correspondences for consonant digraphs (Find a word that has the same sound as the underlined letter or letters in the word. Examples include *bath, skate, smile, black, quick, pond, clap, broke, spot, with, fast, dry, that, bump.*)	
Decodes one-syllable words, such as *mat, tan, peg, web, bud, hop, jig, kit, shop, wish, chat, much, think, moth, when, trip, jolt, bend, bike, late*	
Knows final –e and common vowel teams for representing long-vowel sounds	
Determines the number of syllables in words, knowing that syllables must have a vowel (Ask, "How many syllables do you see in . . . ?")	
Decodes two-syllable words by breaking the words into syllables.	
Reads words with inflectional endings (Ask, "Which word has the same sound as the underlined parts of _____?" such as *ask-asked-asking, jumps-jump-jumped-jumping, looked-looking-looks-look.*)	
Reads irregularly spelled words (*the, have, said, come, give, of, teacher, watched, present, people*)	
Reads high-frequency words from list and in context	
Reads with the fluency (accuracy, rate, and expression) to comprehend	
Reads connected text at a rate of forty to sixty words correct per minute	
Reads with correct pacing (matching natural speech)	
Reads at an appropriate volume	
Observes punctuation marks (pauses when appropriate)	
Is able to figure out difficult words	
Reads with expression (indicating comprehension)	
Uses context to confirm, self-correct, and understand	

Comprehension and Vocabulary		
Asks and answers questions about key details		
Identifies the main topic and retells key details		
Identifies the reasons an author gives to support points		
Identifies words and phrases that suggest feelings or appeal to the senses		
Identifies who is telling the story at various points		
Describes characters using key details from illustrations and written details		
Describes settings using key details from illustrations and written details		
Describes major events using key details from illustrations and written details		
Explains differences between books that tell stories and books that give information		
Compares and contrasts: • Adventures and experiences of characters • Illustrations, descriptions, or procedures • Two individuals, events, ideas, or pieces of information		
Uses text features (headings, tables of contents, glossaries, electronic menus, icons)		
Asks and answers questions to help clarify the meaning of words and phrases		

RTI in the Early Grades © 2013 Solution Tree Press • solution-tree.com
Visit **go.solution-tree.com/rti** to download this page.

Second-Grade Monitoring Tool

Skills	Teacher Notes
Phonics and Fluency	
Distinguishes long and short vowels in one-syllable words	
Knows spelling-sound correspondences for vowel teams	
Decodes two-syllable words with long vowels	
Decodes words with common prefixes and suffixes	
Reads irregularly spelled words	
Reads with the accuracy and fluency to comprehend	
Reads text orally with accuracy, rate, and expression	
Uses context to confirm, self-correct, and understand	
Comprehension and Vocabulary	
Asks and answers such questions as who, what, where, when, why, and how to demonstrate understanding of key details	
Recounts stories (fables or folktales from diverse cultures) and determines their moral	
Identifies the main topic of a multiparagraph text and the focus of paragraphs	
Describes how characters respond to major events and challenges	
Describes how words and phrases (such as regular beats, alliteration, rhymes, repeated lines) supply rhythm and meaning in a story, poem, or song	
Describes the structure of a story—how the beginning introduces and the ending concludes	
Uses text features (such as captions, bold print, subheadings, glossaries, indexes, electronic menus, icons)	
Uses images, diagrams, illustrations, and words to comprehend characters	
Uses images, diagrams, illustrations, and words to comprehend settings	

page 1 of 2

Uses images, diagrams, illustrations, and words to comprehend plots	
Describes connections between historical events, scientific ideas, and steps	
Compares and contrasts: • Two or more versions of the same story by different authors or from different cultures • The most important points in two texts on the same topic	
Determines the meaning of words and phrases	
Identifies the main purpose—what the author wants to answer, explain, or describe	
Acknowledges points of view of characters, speaking in a different voice when reading dialogue aloud	
Comprehends literature and informational texts (social studies, science, technical)	

RTI in the Early Grades © 2013 Solution Tree Press • solution-tree.com

Visit **go.solution-tree.com/rti** to download this page.

Third-Grade Monitoring Tool

Skills	Teacher Notes
Phonics and Fluency	
Knows the meaning of common prefixes and derivational suffixes	
Decodes words with common Latin suffixes	
Decodes multisyllabic words	
Reads irregularly spelled words	
Reads with the accuracy and fluency to comprehend	
Reads text orally with accuracy, rate, and expression	
Uses context to confirm, self-correct, and understand	
Comprehension and Vocabulary	
Asks and answers questions to demonstrate understanding, referring explicitly to text	
Determines the main idea of a text; explains how key details support the main idea	
Recounts stories (fables and folktales from diverse cultures) and determines their moral; explains how it is conveyed through key details	
Describes characters and explains how their actions contribute to the sequence of events	
Refers to parts of stories, dramas, and poems, using chapter, scene, and stanza	
Describes connections between sentences and paragraphs (comparison, cause/effect, and sequence)	
Uses information from illustrations to demonstrate understanding (where, when, why, and how events occur)	
Describes connections between historical events, scientific ideas, and steps, using language that pertains to sequence and cause/effect	

RTI in the Early Grades © 2013 Solution Tree Press • solution-tree.com

Visit **go.solution-tree.com/rti** to download this page.

Compares and contrasts: • Themes, settings, and plots of stories written by the same author about the same or similar characters (such as in books from a series) • Important points and key details presented in two texts on the same topic	
Determines the meaning of general academic and domain-specific words and phrases	
Distinguishes literal from nonliteral language	
Uses text features and search tools to locate information	
Distinguishes the reader's point of view from the author's, narrator's, or character's	
Comprehends literature and informational texts (social studies, science, technical)	

RTI in the Early Grades © 2013 Solution Tree Press • solution-tree.com
Visit **go.solution-tree.com/rti** to download this page.

Upper- and Lowercase Letters Monitoring Tool

Use this tool as you assess student knowledge of letter names and sounds. Use it several times throughout the year, perhaps with different colored pens, to show changes in student performance. Student knowledge of all letter names and sounds is the goal.

S	m	r	T	B	n	v	H	t	V	Z
c	A	p	G	F	q	L	l	i	O	E
z	l	o	C	K	a	w	X	k	W	d
D	R	e	J	h	U	M	B	j	b	y
u	Q	X	N	P	g	s	F	x	Y	f

Sample English Language Development Lesson for Second Grade

Language Function	Express needs and make requests	Express feelings, ideas, and preferences
Grammar Forms	Questions and statements with auxiliary verbs: *may, can, will*	*Don't* + verb: *like, want, enjoy* Conjunctions: *because, when*
Objective	I can use auxiliary verbs in order to express needs and make requests.	I can use *don't* + verb and conjunctions in order to express feelings and preferences.
Topic	Classroom materials and procedures	Playground situations
Prompts and Responses	Can you please hand me the _____? Can you please hand me the (stapler)? Will you please give me the _____? Will you please give me the (staplers)? Here is the _____. Here is the (stapler). Here are the _____. Here are the (staplers). May I go to the _____? May I go to the (library)? Yes, you may go to the _____. Yes, you may go to the (library). No, you may not go to the _____. No, you may not go to the (library).	What do you like to play at recess? I like to play _____ at recess because _____. I like to play (on the playground) at recess because (it's fun). I don't like to play _____ at recess because _____. I don't like to play (on the playground) at recess because (it's boring). Where do you enjoy playing at recess? I enjoy playing _____ at recess when _____. I enjoy playing (on the playground) at recess when (it's sunny). I don't enjoy playing _____ at recess when _____. I don't enjoy playing (on the playground) at recess when (it's cold). What do you want to play during recess? I want to play _____ during recess. I want to play (catch) during recess. I don't want to play _____ during recess. I don't want to play (catch) during recess.

page 1 of 2

RTI in the Early Grades © 2013 Solution Tree Press • solution-tree.com

Visit **go.solution-tree.com/rti** to download this page.

Vocabulary	book stapler ruler paperclip Scotch tape masking tape crayon dictionary journal notebook	pen marker social studies book science book math book glue paper English book textbook novel	classroom cafeteria bathroom library gym office playground	on the playground on the slide handball soccer on the blacktop on the swings	basketball jump rope snack on the monkey bars four-square tetherball football freeze tag	it's fun it's boring it's hard it's scary it's sunny it's hot it's cold it's raining
Application	Students will write a simple play, with six exchanges between two friends who are asking one another for classroom materials.			Students will write a narrative paragraph describing their preferred recess activities.		

Sample English Language Development Lesson for Third Grade

Language Function	Discuss prior experiences	Relate a past action occurring with some other event
Grammar Forms	Present perfect positive and negative questions and statements with auxiliary verbs: *have, has*	Past continuous: *was/were* + verb -ing
Objective	I can use present perfect and auxiliary verbs to discuss prior experiences.	I can use past continuous verbs to relate a past action with some other event.
Topic	Travel and transportation	Animals
Prompts and Responses	Have you/they ever _____ in/on a/an _____? Yes, I/they have _____ in/on a/an _____. No, I/they haven't ever _____ in/on a/an _____. Has she/he ever _____ in/on a/an _____? Yes, he/she has _____ in/on a/an _____. No, he/she hasn't ever _____ in/on a/an _____.	_____, while I _____, a(n) _____ was _____ -ing. _____, while I _____, _____ were _____ -ing. _____, while I _____, the _____ was _____ -ing. _____, while I _____, the _____ were _____ -ing.

Vocabulary						
sat	tow truck	yesterday	took a bath	cat	bark
ridden	ambulance	last year		kitten	meow
traveled	sailboat	last night	watched TV	bird	neigh
stood	skateboard	last week	read a book	eagle	gallop
lounged	airport	this morning		falcon	crawl
snacked	airplane		played with my friends	raven	hop
slept	covered wagon			horse	jump

page 1 of 2

Vocabulary		space shuttle		ate dinner	mare	float
		stroller			colt	run
		taxi		brushed my teeth	foal	swim
		train			amphibian	spin
		helicopter			frog	speed
		dump truck			toad	dash
					salamander	glide
					dog	torpedo
					Dalmatian	soar
					Chihuahua	sink
					sea animal	dive
					dolphin	die
					whale	canter
					fish	whinny
					shark	
Application		Students will "find someone who . . ." and construct a tree map, which they will share out in complete sentences with their group and class.		Students will write a five-sentence narrative describing a favorite animal.		

Check-In/Check-Out Monitoring Tool

Check-In/Check-Out for:		Date:
Check-In/Check-Out with:		

Today, I am working on:

This is how I did today:

3 = Great!	**2 = Pretty Good**	**1 = So-So**
(I was reminded to be on-task 1 or 0 times.)	(I was reminded to be on-task 3 or 2 times.)	(I was reminded to be on-task more than 3 times.)

Time of Day	Staying on Task (Student)	Staff	

REFERENCES AND RESOURCES

Adams, M. J. (1990). *Beginning to read: Thinking and learning about print.* Cambridge, MA: MIT Press.

Adams, M. J., Foorman, B. R., Lundberg, I., & Beeler, T. (1998). *Phonemic awareness in young children.* Baltimore: Brookes.

Adger, C. T., Snow, C. E., & Christian, D. (Eds.). (2002). *What teachers need to know about language.* McHenry, IL: Delta Systems.

Ainsworth, L. (2003a). *Power standards: Identifying the standards that matter the most.* Denver, CO: Advanced Learning Press.

Ainsworth, L. (2003b). *"Unwrapping" the standards: A simple process to make standards manageable.* Denver, CO: Advanced Learning Press.

Ainsworth, L., & Christinson, J. (2006). *Five easy steps to a balanced math program for primary grades: Grades K–2.* Englewood, CO: Lead and Learn Press.

Allington, R. L. (2001). *What really matters for struggling readers: Designing research-based programs.* New York: Addison-Wesley.

Allington, R. L. (2002). You can't learn much from books you can't read. *Educational Leadership, 60*(3), 16–19.

Allington, R. L. (2009). *What really matters in response to intervention: Research-based designs.* Boston: Allyn & Bacon.

Allington, R. L., & Cunningham, P. M. (2002). *Schools that work: Where all children read and write* (2nd ed.). Boston: Allyn & Bacon.

Allington, R. L., & Gabriel, R. E. (2012). Every child, every day. *Educational Leadership, 69*(6), 10–15.

American Diploma Project. (2004). *Ready or not: Creating a high school diploma that counts.* Washington, DC: Achieve.

August, D., & Shanahan, T. (Eds.). (2006). *Developing literacy in second-language learners: A report of the National Literacy Panel on Language-Minority Children and Youth.* Mahwah, NJ: Erlbaum.

Auman, M. (2003). *Step up to writing.* Longmont, CO: Sopris West.

Baker, S., Gersten, R., & Lee, D. S. (2002). A synthesis of empirical research on teaching mathematics to low-achieving students. *Elementary School Journal, 103*(1), 51–73.

Ball, D. L., Ferrini-Mundy, J., Kilpatrick, J., Milgram, R. J., Schmid, W., & Schaar, R. (2009). Reaching for common ground in K–12 mathematics education. *Notices of the American Mathematical Society, 52*(9), 1055–1058.

Barnett, W. S. (2002). Kindergarten education for economically disadvantaged children: Effects on reading achievement and related outcomes. In S. Neuman & D. K. Dickinson (Eds.), *Handbook of early literacy* (pp. 421–443). New York: Guilford Press.

Barrish, B. (1970). *Inductive versus deductive teaching strategies with high and low divergent thinkers.* Palo Alto, CA: Stanford University Press.

Barth, R. (1991). Restructuring schools: Some questions for teachers and principals. *Phi Delta Kappan, 73*(2), 123–128.

Battista, M. T. (1999). The mathematical miseducation of America's youth: Ignoring research and scientific study in education. *Phi Delta Kappan, 80,* 424–433.

Bear, D. R., Invernizzi, M., Templeton, S., & Johnston, F. (2000). *Words their way: Word study for phonics, vocabulary, and spelling instruction* (2nd ed.). Upper Saddle River, NJ: Prentice Hall.

Beck, I. L., McKeown, M. G., & Kucan, L. (2002). *Bringing words to life: Robust vocabulary instruction.* New York: Guilford Press.

Bellanca, J., & Brandt, R. (Eds.). (2010). *21st century skills: Rethinking how students learn.* Bloomington, IN: Solution Tree Press.

Berninger, V. W., & Rutberg, J. (1992). Relationship of finger function to beginning writing: Application to diagnosis of writing disabilities. *Developmental Medicine and Child Neurology, 34,* 198–215.

Berninger, V. W., Vaughan, K. B., Abbott, R. D., Abbott, S. P., Rogan, L. W., Brooks, A., et al. (1997). Treatment of handwriting problems in beginning writers: Transfer from handwriting to composition. *Journal of Educational Psychology, 89,* 652–666.

Black, P., & Wiliam, D. (1998). Inside the black box: Raising standards through classroom assessment. *Phi Delta Kappan, 80*(2), 139–148.

Bowman, B., Donovan, M. S., & Burns, M. S. (Eds.). (2000). *Eager to learn: Educating our kindergarteners.* Washington, DC: National Academies Press.

Brien, T. C. (1999). Parrot math. *Phi Delta Kappan, 80,* 434–443.

Brock, S. E. (1998). Helping the student with ADHD in the classroom: Strategies for teachers. *Communiqué, 26*(5), 18–20.

Bryant, D. P., Bryant, B. R., Gersten, R., Scammacca, N., & Chavez, M. (2008). Mathematics intervention for first and second grade students with mathematics difficulties: The effects of tier 2 intervention delivered as booster lessons. *Remedial and Special Education, 29*(1), 20–32.

Buckner, J. C. (2000). *Write from the beginning.* Cary, NC: Thinking Maps.

Buffum, A., Mattos, M., & Weber, C. (2009). *Pyramid response to intervention: RTI, professional learning communities, and how to respond when kids don't learn.* Bloomington, IN: Solution Tree Press.

Buffum, A., Mattos, M., & Weber, C. (2010). The why behind RTI. *Educational Leadership, 68*(2), 10–16.

Buffum, A., Mattos, M., & Weber, C. (2012). *Simplifying response to intervention: Four essential guiding principles.* Bloomington, IN: Solution Tree Press.

Bull, R., & Johnston, R. J. (1997). Children's arithmetical difficulties: Contributions from processing speed, item identification, and short-term memory. *Journal of Experimental Child Psychology, 65,* 1–24.

Burke, M. D., Hagan-Burke, S., Kwok, O., & Parker, R. (2009). Predictive validity of early literacy indicators from the middle of kindergarten to second grade. *Journal of Special Education, 42*(4), 209–226.

Burns, P. C., Roe, B. D., & Ross, E. P. (1996). *Teaching reading in today's elementary schools* (6th ed.). Boston: Houghton Mifflin.

California Department of Education. (n.d.). *Data quest.* Accessed at www.cde.ca.gov/ds/sd/cb /dataquest.asp on January 13, 2012.

California Department of Education. (2002). *English-language development standards for California public schools, kindergarten through grade twelve.* Sacramento, CA: Author.

Calkins, L. M. (1986). *The art of teaching writing.* Portsmouth, NH: Heinemann.

Canale, M., & Swain, M. (1980). Theoretical bases of communicative approaches to second language teaching and testing. *Applied Linguistics, 1,* 1–47.

Carnine, D. W. (1976). Effects of two teacher presentation rates on off-task behavior, answering correctly, and participation. *Journal of Applied Behavior Analysis, 9,* 199–206.

Case-Smith, J. (2002). Effectiveness of school-based occupational therapy intervention on handwriting. *American Journal of Occupational Therapy, 56*(1), 17–25.

Catts, H. W., Fey, M. E., Tomblin, J. B., & Zhang, X. (2002). A longitudinal investigation of reading outcomes in children with language impairments. *Journal of Speech, Language, and Hearing Research, 45,* 1142–1157.

Cazden, C. B. (2001). *Classroom discourse: The language of teaching and learning* (2nd ed.). Portsmouth, NH: Heinemann.

Center for Applied Linguistics. (n.d.). *Structured oral language observation matrix.* Accessed at www.cal.org/twi/evaltoolkit/appendix/solom.pdf on December 19, 2011.

Christinson, J., & Ainsworth, L. (2008). *Five easy steps to a balanced math program for primary grades.* Denver, CO: Lead and Learn Press.

City, E. A., Elmore, R. F., Fiarman, S. E., & Teitel, L. (2009). *Instructional rounds in education: A network approach to improving teaching and learning.* Cambridge, MA: Harvard Education Publishing Group.

Clay, M. M. (1979). *What did I write? Beginning writing behaviour.* Portsmouth, NH: Heinemann.

Collins, J. (2001). *Good to great: Why some companies make the leap . . . and others don't.* New York: HarperCollins.

Collins, J. C., & Porras, J. I. (1994). *Built to last: Successful habits of visionary companies.* New York: HarperCollins.

Connor, C. D., & Tiedemann, P. J. (2005). *International Reading Association—National Institute for Child Health and Human Development Conference on Early Childhood Literacy Research: A summary of presentations and discussions.* Newark, DE: International Reading Association.

Consortium on Reading Excellence. (1999). *Reading research anthology: The why of reading instruction.* Novato, CA: Arena Press.

Consortium on Reading Excellence. (2008). *Assessing reading: Multiple measures for kindergarten through twelfth grade* (2nd ed.). Novato, CA: Arena Press.

Cotton, K. (2003). *Principals and student achievement: What the research says.* Alexandria, VA: Association for Supervision and Curriculum Development.

Coyne, M. D., & Harn, B. A. (2006). Promoting beginning reading success through meaningful assessment of early literacy skills. *Psychology in the Schools, 43*(1), 33–43.

Coyne, M. D., Kame'enui, E. J., & Simmons, D. C. (2004). Improving beginning reading instruction and intervention for students with LD: Reconciling "all" with "each." *Journal of Learning Disabilities, 37*(3), 231–239.

Cummins, J. (1986). Empowering minority students: A framework for intervention. *Harvard Education Review, 56,* 18–36.

Dehaune, S. (1997). *The number sense: How the mind creates mathematics.* Oxford, England: Oxford University Press.

Dickinson, D. K., & Neuman, S. B. (Eds.). (2006). *Handbook of early literacy research* (Vol. 2). New York: Guilford Press.

Doyle, W. (1983). Academic work. *Review of Educational Research, 53*(2), 159–199.

DuFour, R., DuFour, R., & Eaker, R. (2008). *Revisiting professional learning communities at work: New insights for improving schools.* Bloomington, IN: Solution Tree Press.

DuFour, R., DuFour, R., Eaker, R., & Many, T. (2010). *Learning by doing* (2nd ed.). Bloomington, IN: Solution Tree Press.

DuFour, R., & Marzano, R. J. (2011). *Leaders of learning: How district, school, and classroom leaders improve student achievement.* Bloomington, IN: Solution Tree Press.

Duke, N. K., & Pearson, P. D. (2002). Effective practices for developing reading comprehension. In A. E. Farstup & S. J. Samuels (Eds.), *What research has to say about reading instruction* (pp. 205–242). Newark, DE: International Reading Association.

Duncan, G. J., Claessens, A., Huston, A. C., Pagani, L. S., Engel, M., Sexton, H., et al. (2007). School readiness and later achievement. *Developmental Psychology, 43*(6), 1428–1446.

DuPaul, G. J., & Ervin, R. A. (1996). Functional assessment of behaviors related to attention-deficit/hyperactivity disorder: Linking assessment to intervention design. *Behavior Therapy, 27,* 601–622.

Dutro, S. (2008). *Express placement assessment.* San Marcos, CA: E. L. Achieve.

Dutro, S., & Moran, C. (2003). Rethinking English language instruction: An architectural approach. In G. Garcia (Ed.), *English learners: Reaching the highest level of English literacy* (pp. 227–258). Newark, DE: International Reading Association.

Dutro, S., Prestridge, K., & Herrick, J. (2005). *ELD matrix of grammatical forms.* San Marcos, CA: E. L. Achieve.

Dweck, C. S. (2006). *Mindset: The new psychology of success.* New York: Random House.

Dweck, C. S., & Wortman, C. B. (1982). Learned helplessness, anxiety, and achievement motivation: Neglected parallels in cognitive, affective, and coping responses. In H. Krohne & L. Laux (Eds.), *Achievement, stress and anxiety* (pp. 93–125). Washington, DC: Hemisphere.

Dynamic Measurement Group. (2009). *Dynamic Indicators of Basic Early Literacy Skills (DIBELS).* Accessed at https://dibels.uoregon.edu on June 19, 2011.

Edmonds, R. (1979). Effective schools for the urban poor. *Educational Leadership, 37*(1), 15–24.

E. L. Achieve. (2006). *Systematic English language development.* San Marcos, CA: Author.

Elmore, R. (2008). *Improving the instructional core.* Accessed at www.acsa.org/MainMenuCategories/ProfessionalLearning/LeadershipCoaching/Coach-Resources/Imp-Instr-Core.aspx on July 26, 2010.

Elmore, R. (2010). Leading the instructional core: A conversation with Richard Elmore. *In Conversation, 11*(3), 1–12.

Emig, J. (1977). Writing as a mode of learning. *College Composition and Communication, 28*(2), 122–128.

Fisher, D., & Frey, N. (2007). *Checking for understanding: Formative assessment techniques for your classroom.* Alexandria, VA: Association for Supervision and Curriculum Development.

Fisher, D., & Frey, N. (2008). *Better learning through structured teaching: A framework for the gradual release of responsibility.* Alexandria, VA: Association for Supervision and Curriculum Development.

Fisher, D., Frey, N., & Rothenberg, C. (2011). *Implementing RTI with English learners.* Bloomington, IN: Solution Tree Press.

Florida Center for Reading Research. (2011). *Student center activities.* Accessed at www.fcrr.org /curriculum/SCAindex.shtm on July 3, 2011.

Flower, L., & Hayes, J. R. (1981). A cognitive process theory of writing. *College Composition and Communication, 32*(4), 365–387.

Ford, A. D., Olmi, D. J., Edwards, R. P., & Tingstrom, D. H. (2001). The sequential introduction of compliance training components with elementary-aged children in general education classroom settings. *School Psychology Quarterly, 16,* 142–157.

Fountas, I. C., & Pinnell, G. S. (1996). *Guided reading: Good first teaching for all children.* Portsmouth, NH: Heinemann.

Fountas, I. C., & Pinnell, G. S. (2006). *Teaching for comprehending and fluency: Thinking, talking, and writing about reading, K–8.* Portsmouth, NH: Heinemann.

Francis, D., Rivera, M., Lesaux, N., Kieffer, M., & Rivera, H. (2006). *Practical guidelines for the education of English language learners: Research-based recommendations for instruction and academic interventions.* Portsmouth, NH: RMC Research Corporation, Center on Instruction. Accessed at www.centeroninstruction.org/files/ELL1-Interventions.pdf on May 3, 2012.

Francis, D., J., Shaywitz, S. E., Stuebing, K. K., Shaywitz, B. A., & Fletcher, J. M. (1996). Developmental lag versus deficit models of reading disability: A longitudinal, individual growth curves analysis. *Journal of Educational Psychology, 88*(1), 3–17.

Fuchs, L. S., Fuchs, D., Hosp, M. K., & Jenkins, J. R. (2001). Oral reading fluency as an indicator of reading competence: A theoretical, empirical, and historical analysis. *Scientific Studies of Reading, 5*(3), 241–258.

Genzuk, M. (2011). *Specially designed academic instruction in English (SDAIE) for language minority students.* Los Angeles: Center for Multilingual, Multicultural Research. Accessed at www .usc.edu/dept/education/CMMR/DigitalPapers/SDAIE_Genzuk.pdf on May 3, 2012.

Gersten, R., Beckmann, S., Clarke, B., Foegen, A., Marsh, L., Star, J. R., et al. (2009). *Assisting students struggling with mathematics: Response to intervention (RtI) for elementary and middle schools* (NCEE 2009-4060). Washington, DC: U.S. Department of Education. Accessed at www.opi.mt.gov/pub/RTI/Training/IESMathPracticeGuide.pdf on February 12, 2012.

Gersten, R., & Chard, D. J. (1999). Number sense: Rethinking arithmetic instruction for students with mathematical disabilities. *Journal of Special Education, 33,* 18–28.

Gersten, R., Chard, D., Jayanthi, M., Baker, S., Morphy, P., & Flojo, J. (2008). *Mathematics instruction for students with learning disabilities or difficulty learning mathematics: A synthesis of the intervention research.* Portsmouth, NH: RMC Research Corporation, Center on Instruction.

Gersten, R., Clarke, B., Haymond, K., & Jordan, N. (2011). *Screening for mathematics difficulties in K–3 students* (2nd ed.). Portsmouth, NH: RMC Research Corporation, Center on Instruction.

Gersten, R., Jordan, N. C., & Flojo, J. (2005). Early identification and interventions for students with mathematics difficulties. *Journal of Learning Disabilities, 38,* 293–304.

Gettinger, M. (1988). Methods of proactive classroom management. *School Psychology Review, 17,* 227–242.

Gettinger, M., & Seibert, J. K. (2002). Best practices in increasing academic learning time. In A. Thomas (Ed.), *Best practices in school psychology IV* (Vol. 1, 4th ed., pp. 773–787). Bethesda, MD: National Association of School Psychologists.

Ginsburg, A., Leinwand, S., Anstrom, T., & Pollock, E. (2005). *What the United States can learn from Singapore's world-class mathematics system (and what Singapore can learn from the United States): An exploratory study.* Washington, DC: American Institutes for Research.

Goldman, K. S. (2005). DIBELS: The perfect literacy test. *Language Magazine, 5*(1), 24–27.

Goldman, K. S. (2006). *The truth about DIBELS: What it is, what it does.* Portsmouth, NH: Heinemann.

Gonzales, P., Williams, T., Jocelyn, L., Roey, S., Kastberg, D., & Brenwald, S. (2008). *Highlights from TIMSS 2007: Mathematics and science achievement of U.S. fourth- and eighth-grade students in an international context* (NCES 2009-001 Revised). Washington, DC: National Center for Education Statistics.

Good, R. H., & Kaminski, R. A. (Eds.). (2002). *Dynamic Indicators of Basic Early Literacy Skills* (6th ed.). Eugene, OR: Institute for Development of Educational Achievement.

Graham, S., & Hebert, M. A. (2010). *Writing to read: Evidence for how writing can improve reading—A Carnegie Corporation Time to Act report.* Washington, DC: Alliance for Excellent Education.

Graham, S., & Perin, D. (2007). *Writing next: Effective strategies to improve writing of adolescents in middle and high schools—A report to Carnegie Corporation of New York.* Washington, DC: Alliance for Excellent Education.

Guided Language Acquisition Design. (n.d.). *What is Project GLAD?* Accessed at www.projectglad.com on November 12, 2011.

Hall, S. J. (2006). *I've DIBEL'd, now what? Designing interventions with DIBELS data.* Dallas, TX: Cambium Learning Group.

Halpern, R. (1999). After-school programs for low-income children: Promise and challenges. *The Future of Children, 9*(2), 81–95.

Hanushek, E. A., Jamison, D. T., Jamison, E. A., & Woessmann, L. (2008). Education and economic growth: It's not just going to school, but learning something while there that matters. *Education Next, 8*(2), 62–70.

Hanushek, E. A., Peterson, P. E., & Woessmann, L. (2011). Teaching math to the talented: Which countries—and states—are producing high-achieving students? *Education Next, 11*(1), 10–18.

Harris, P. (2006). Writing boosts learning in science, math, and social studies. *Council Chronicle, 16*(1).

Hattie, J. (2009). *Visible learning: A synthesis of over 800 meta-analyses relating to student achievement.* New York: Routledge.

Heckman, J. J. (2006, January). *Investing in disadvantaged young children is an economically efficient policy.* Presented at the Committee for Economic Development/Pew Charitable Trusts/PNC Financial Services Group Forum on Building the Case for Economic Investments in Preschool, New York, NY.

Heward, W. L. (1994). Three "low-tech" strategies for increasing the frequency of active student response during group instruction. In R. Gardner III, D. M. Sainato, J. O. Cooper, T. E. Heron, W. L. Heward, J. Eshleman, et al. (Eds.), *Behavior analysis in education: Focus on measurably superior instruction* (pp. 283–320). Monterey, CA: Brooks/Cole.

Hiebert, J. (1999). Relationships between research and the NCTM Standards. *Journal for Research in Mathematics Education, 30,* 3–19.

Higgins, L. (2008, May 27). Algebra I stumping high school freshmen: Class of 2011 confronts tougher state requirements. *Detroit Free Press*, p. A3.

Hollingsworth, J., & Ybarra, S. (2009). *Explicit direction instruction (EDI): The power of the well-crafted, well-taught lesson.* Thousand Oaks, CA: Corwin Press.

Hook, P. E., & Jones, S. D. (2004). The importance of automaticity and fluency for efficient reading comprehension. *Perspectives on Language and Literacy, 28*(1), 9–14.

Howes, C. (Ed.). (2003). *Teaching 4- to 8-year-olds literacy, math, multiculturalism and classroom community.* Baltimore: Brookes.

Hunter, M. (1982). *Mastery teaching.* El Segundo, CA: TIP Publications.

Intervention Central. (2011). *Academic interventions.* Accessed at www.interventioncentral.org /academic-interventions/ on July 3, 2011.

Jayanthi, M., Gersten, R., & Baker, S. (2008). *Mathematics instruction for students with learning disabilities or difficulty learning mathematics: A guide for teachers.* Portsmouth, NH: Instructional Research Group, Center on Instruction.

Jordan, N. C., Kaplan, D., Olah, L. N., & Locuniak, M. N. (2006). Number sense growth in kindergarten: A longitudinal investigation of children at risk for mathematics difficulties. *Child Development, 77*, 153–175.

Jordan, N. C., Kaplan, D., Ramineni, C., & Locuniak, M. N. (2009). Early math matters: Kindergarten number competence and later mathematics outcomes. *Developmental Psychology, 45*, 850–867.

Jordan, N. C., Levine, S., & Huttenlocher, J. (1994). Development of calculation abilities in middle and low-income children after formal instruction in school. *Journal of Applied Developmental Psychology, 15*, 223–240.

Joyce, B., & Weil, M. (1972). *Models of teaching.* Boston: Allyn & Bacon.

Juel, C. (1988). Learning to read and write: A longitudinal study of 54 children from first to fourth grades. *Journal of Educational Psychology, 80*(4), 437–447.

Kalchman, M., Moss, J., & Case, R. (2001). Psychological models for the development of mathematical understanding: Rational numbers and functions. In S. Carver & D. Klahr (Eds.), *Cognition and instruction* (pp. 1–38). Mahwah, NJ: Erlbaum.

Kane, T. J. (2004). *The impact of after-school programs: Interpreting the results of four recent evaluations* [William T. Grant Foundation Working Paper]. New York: William T. Grant Foundation.

Karoly, L. A., Kilburn, M. R., & Cannon, J. S. (2005). *Early childhood interventions: Proven results, future promises.* Arlington, VA: RAND Corporation.

Keene, E. O., & Zimmermann, S. (1997). *Mosaic of thought: Teaching comprehension in a reader's workshop.* Portsmouth, NH: Heinemann.

Kern, R. (2000). *Literacy and language teaching.* Hong Kong: Oxford University Press.

Khan, C., & Mellard, D. (2008). *RTI in the language of the classroom teacher: Improving student success through collaboration.* Lawrence, KS: National Center on Response to Intervention.

Kinsella, K. (2005, November). Teaching academic vocabulary. *Aiming High,* 1–3, 6–8.

Kloosterman, P. (2010). Mathematics skills of 17-year-olds in the United States: 1978 to 2004. *Journal for Research in Mathematics Education, 41*, 20–51.

Krashen, S. D. (1985). *Inquiries & insight: Second language teaching, immersion & bilingual education.* Hayward, CA: Alemany Press.

Krashen, S. D., & Terrell, T. D. (1983). *The natural approach: Language acquisition in the classroom.* Hayward, CA: Alemany Press.

Lee, J. S., & Oxelson, E. (2006). "It's not my job": K–12 teacher attitude toward students' heritage language maintenance. *Bilingual Research Journal, 30*, 453–477.

Leithwood, K., Anderson, S., Mascall, B., & Strauss, T. (2010). School leaders' influences on student learning: The four paths. In T. Bush, L. Bell, & D. Middlewood (Eds.), *The principles of educational leadership and management*. London: SAGE.

Leithwood, K., McAdie, P., Bascia, N., & Rodrigue, A. (2005). *Teaching for deep understanding: What every educator should know*. Thousand Oaks, CA: Corwin Press.

Lembke, E. S., & Foegen, A. (2009). Identifying early numeracy indicators for kindergarten and grade 1 students. *Learning Disabilities Research & Practice, 24*, 12–20.

Lembke, E. S., & Stecker, P. (2007). *Curriculum-based measurement in mathematics: An evidence-based formative assessment procedure*. Portsmouth, NH: RMC Research Corporation, Center on Instruction.

Leslie, L., & Caldwell, J. S. (2011). *Qualitative reading inventory-5*. Boston: Allyn & Bacon.

Light, G. J., & DeFries, J. C. (1995). Comorbidity of reading and mathematics disabilities: Genetic and environmental etiologies. *Journal of Learning Disabilities, 28*, 96–106.

Locuniak, M. N., & Jordan, N. C. (2008). Using kindergarten number sense to predict calculation fluency in second grade. *Journal of Learning Disabilities, 41*, 451–459.

Lucas, T., & Katz, A. (1994). Reforming the debate: The roles of native languages in English-only programs for language minority students. *TESOL Quarterly, 28*(3), 538–561.

Lyman, F. T. (1981). The responsive classroom discourse: The inclusion of all students. In A. Anderson (Ed.), *Mainstreaming digest* (pp. 109–113). College Park: University of Maryland Press.

Lyon, G. R., Fletcher, J. M., Shaywitz, S. E., Shaywitz, B. A., Torgesen, J. K., Wood, F. B., et al. (2001). Rethinking learning disabilities. In C. E. Finn, A. J. Rotherham, & C. R. Hokanson (Eds.), *Rethinking special education for a new century* (pp. 259–287). Washington, DC: Progressive Policy Institute/Thomas B. Fordham Foundation.

Martens, B. K., & Kelly, S. Q. (1993). A behavioral analysis of effective teaching. *School Psychology Quarterly, 8*, 10–26.

Martens, B. K., & Meller, P. J. (1990). The application of behavioral principles to educational settings. In T. B. Gutkin & C. R. Reynolds (Eds.), *The handbook of school psychology* (2nd ed., pp. 612–634). New York: Wiley.

Marzano, R. J. (2003). *What works in schools: Translating research into action*. Alexandria, VA: Association for Supervision and Curriculum Development.

Marzano, R. J. (2006). *Classroom assessment and grading that work*. Alexandria, VA: Association for Supervision and Curriculum Development.

Marzano, R. J., Pickering, D. J., & Pollock, J. E. (2001). *Classroom instruction that works: Research-based strategies for increasing student achievement*. Alexandria, VA: Association for Supervision and Curriculum Development.

Marzano, R. J., Waters, T., & McNulty, B. A. (2005). *School leadership that works: From research to results*. Alexandria, VA: Association for Supervision and Curriculum Development.

Mazzocco, M., & Thompson, R. E. (2005). Kindergarten predictors of math learning disability. *Learning Disabilities Research & Practice, 20*, 142–155.

McEwan, E. K. (1998). *Seven steps to effective instructional leadership*. Thousand Oaks, CA: Corwin Press.

McEwan-Adkins, E. K. (2010). *40 reading intervention strategies for K–6 students: Research-based support for RTI*. Bloomington, IN: Solution Tree Press.

McIntosh, K., Chard, D. J., Boland, J. B., & Horner, R. H. (2006). Demonstration of combined efforts in school-wide academic and behavioral systems and incidence of reading and behavior challenges in early elementary grades. *Journal of Positive Behavior Interventions, 8*, 146–154.

McLaughlin, B. (1985). *Second language acquisition in childhood* (Vol. 2). Hillsdale, NJ: Lawrence Erlbaum Associates.

Mercer, C. D., Campbell, K. U., Miller, D., Mercer, K. D., & Lane, H. B. (2000). Effects of a reading fluency intervention for middle schoolers with specific learning disabilities. *Learning Disabilities Research & Practice, 15*(4), 179–189.

Methe, S. A., Hintze, J. M., & Floyd, R. G. (2008). Development and validation of early numeracy skill indicators. *School Psychology Review, 37*, 359–373.

Milgram, R. J. (2006, November). *The mathematics teachers need to know*. Presented at the Center on Instruction Mathematics Summit, Annapolis, MD.

Miller, D. (2002). *Reading with meaning: Teaching comprehension in the primary grades*. Portland, ME: Stenhouse.

Miller, S. P., & Hudson, P. J. (2007). Using evidence-based practices to build mathematics competence related to conceptual, procedural, and declarative knowledge. *Learning Disabilities Research & Practice, 22*(1), 47–57.

Morgan, P. L., Farkas, G., & Wu, Q. (2009). Five-year growth trajectories of kindergarten children with learning difficulties in mathematics. *Journal of Learning Disabilities, 42*, 306–321.

Moss, B. (2004). Teaching expository text structures through information trade book retellings. *Reading Teacher, 57*(8), 710–718.

Moughamian, A. C., Rivera, M. O., & Francis, D. J. (2009). *Instructional models and strategies for teaching English language learners*. Portsmouth, NH: RMC Research Corporation, Center on Instruction.

Mullis, I. V. S., Martin, M. O., Olson, J. F., Berger, D. R., Milne, D., & Stanco, G. M. (Eds.). (2007). *TIMSS 2007 encyclopedia: A guide to mathematics and science education around the world* (Vols. 1 & 2). Chestnut Hill, MA: TIMSS and PIRLS International Study Center.

National Center for Education Statistics. (2010). *The condition of education 2010*. Washington, DC: Author.

National Commission on Excellence in Education. (1983). *A nation at risk: The imperative for educational reform*. Washington, DC: U.S. Department of Education.

National Council of Teachers of English, & International Reading Association. (2011). *Classroom resources*. Accessed at www.readwritethink.org/classroom-resources on July 3, 2011.

National Governors Association Center for Best Practices, & Council of Chief State School Officers. (2010a). *Common Core State Standards for English language arts & literacy in history/social studies, science, and technical subjects*. Washington, DC: Author. Accessed at www .corestandards.org/assets/CCSSI_ELA%20Standards.pdf on July 6, 2012.

National Governors Association Center for Best Practices, & Council of Chief State School Officers. (2010b). *Common Core State Standards for mathematics*. Washington, DC: Author. Accessed at www.corestandards.org/assets/CCSSI_Math%20Standards.pdf on July 6, 2012.

National Institute of Child Health and Human Development. (2000). *Report of the National Reading Panel: Teaching children to read—An evidence-based assessment of the scientific research literature on reading and its implications for reading instruction—Reports of the subgroups* (NIH Publication No. 00-4754). Washington, DC: U.S. Government Printing Office.

National Institute of Child Health and Human Development. (2001). *Put reading first: The research building blocks for teaching children to read*. Washington, DC: U.S. Government Printing Office.

National Institute of Child Health and Human Development Early Child Care Research Network. (2005). Pathways to reading: The role of oral language in the transition to reading. *Developmental Psychology, 41*, 428–442.

National Institute for Literacy. (2008). *Developing early literacy: Report of the National Early Literacy Panel—A scientific synthesis of early literacy development and implications for intervention*. Washington, DC: U.S. Government Printing Office.

National Mathematics Advisory Panel. (2008). *Foundations for success: The final report of the National Mathematics Advisory Panel*. Washington, DC: U.S. Department of Education.

National Research Council. (1998). *Preventing reading difficulties in young children*. Washington, DC: National Academies Press.

National Research Council. (2001). *Adding it up: Helping children learn mathematics*. Washington, DC: National Academies Press.

Newman-Gonchar, R., Clarke, B., & Gersten, R. (2009). *Multi-tier intervention and response to interventions for students struggling in mathematics: A summary of nine key studies*. Portsmouth, NH: RMC Research Corporation, Center on Instruction.

Newmann, F. M., & Wehlage, G. G. (1993). Five standards of authentic instruction. *Educational Leadership, 50*(7), 8–12.

No Child Left Behind Act of 2001, Pub. L. No. 107-110, § 5, 115 Stat. 1427 *et seq.* (2002).

Norris, J. M., & Ortega, L. (2006). The value and practice of research synthesis for language learning and teaching. In J. M. Norris & L. Ortega (Eds.), *Synthesizing research on language learning and teaching* (pp. 3–50). Amsterdam: John Benjamins.

Northwest Regional Educational Laboratory. (1999). *Seeing with new eyes: A guidebook on teaching and assessing beginning writers using the six-trait writing model* (5th ed.). Portland, OR: Author.

Okamoto, Y., & Case, R. (1996). Exploring the microstructure of children's central conceptual structures in the domain of number. *Monographs of the Society for Research in Child Development, 61*, 27–58.

Oregon Reading First Center. (2011). *Curriculum review.* Accessed at http://oregonreadingfirst .uoregon.edu/inst_curr_review_si.html on July 3, 2011.

Organisation for Economic Co-operation and Development. (2011). *Strong performers and successful reformers in education: Lessons from PISA for the United States.* Paris: Author. Accessed at www.oecd.org/dataoecd/32/50/46623978.pdf on May 3, 2012.

Pashler, H., Bain, P. M., McDaniel, M., Bottge, B. A., Graesser, A., Koedinger, K., et al. (2008). *Organizing instruction and study to improve student learning: IES practice guide* (NCES 2007–2004). Washington, DC: Institute of Education Sciences.

Pearson, P. D., & Gallagher, G. (1983). The gradual release of responsibility model of instruction. *Contemporary Educational Psychology, 8*, 112–123.

Peters, T. J., & Waterman, R. H., Jr. (1982). *In search of excellence: Lessons from America's best-run companies.* New York: HarperCollins.

Posner, J. K., & Vandell, D. L. (1994). Low-income children's after-school care: Are there beneficial effects of after-school programs? *Child Development, 65*(2), 440–456.

Powell, S., & Nelson, B. (1997). Effects of choosing academic assignments on a student with attention deficit hyperactivity disorder. *Journal of Applied Behavior Analysis, 30*, 181–183.

Pressley, M. (1998). *Reading instruction that works: The case for balanced teaching.* New York: Guilford Press.

Reading by 9: A *Los Angeles Times* child literacy initiative. (n.d.). Accessed at www.latimes.com /extras/readingby9 on June 18, 2011.

Reeves, D. (2000). *Accountability in action: A blueprint for learning organizations.* Denver, CO: Advanced Learning Centers.

Reeves, D. (2002). *The leader's guide to standards: A blueprint for educational equity and excellence.* San Francisco: Wiley.

Rittle-Johnson, B., Siegler, R. S., & Alibali, M. W. (2001). Developing conceptual understanding and procedural skill in mathematics: An iterative process. *Journal of Educational Psychology, 93*(2), 346–362.

Rivera, M. O., Moughamian, A. C., Lesaux, N. K., & Francis, D. J. (2008). *Language and reading interventions for English language learners and English language learners with disabilities.* Portsmouth, NH: RMC Research Corporation, Center on Instruction.

Robinson, V. B., Ross, G., & Neal, H. C. (2000). *Emergent literacy in kindergarten: A review of the research and related suggested activities and learning strategies.* San Mateo, CA: California Kindergarten Association.

Routman, R. (2002). *Reading essentials: The specifics you need to teach reading well.* Portsmouth, NH: Heinemann.

Routman, R. (2004). *Writing essentials: Raising expectations and results while simplifying teaching.* Portsmouth, NH: Heinemann.

Routman, R. (2007). *Teaching essentials: Expecting the most and getting the best from every learner, K–8.* Portsmouth, NH: Heinemann.

Saunders, W. M., Foorman, B. R., & Carlson, C. D. (2006). Is a separate block of time for oral English language development in programs for English learners needed? *Elementary School Journal, 107*(2), 181–198.

Saunders, W., & Goldenberg, C. (2010). Research to guide English language development instruction. In Center for Applied Linguistics, *Improving education for English learners: Research-based approaches* (pp. 24–81). Sacramento: California Department of Education.

Scarcella, R. C. (1996). Secondary education and second language research: Instructing ESL students in the 1990s. *CATESOL Journal, 9,* 129–152.

Scarcella, R. (2003). *Accelerating academic English: A focus on English language learners.* Oakland: Regents of the University of California.

Scherer, M. (2001). How and why standards can improve student achievement: A conversation with Robert J. Marzano. *Educational Leadership, 59*(1), 14–18.

Schielack, J., Charles, R., Clements, D., Duckett, P., Fennell, F., Lawandowski, S., et al. (Eds.). (2006). *Curriculum focal points for prekindergarten through grade 8 mathematics: A quest for coherence.* Reston, VA: National Council of Teachers of Mathematics.

Schlechty, P. C. (2002). *Working on the work: An action plan for teachers, principals, and superintendents.* San Francisco: Jossey-Bass.

Schoen, H. L., Fey, J. T., Hirsch, C. R., & Coxford, A. F. (1999). Issues and options in the math wars. *Phi Delta Kappan, 80,* 444–453.

Shaywitz, S. E. (2003). *Overcoming dyslexia.* New York: Knopf.

Shaywitz, S. E., Fletcher, J. M., Holahan, J. M., Schneider, A. E., Marchione, K. E., Stuebing, K. K., et al. (1999). Persistence of dyslexia: The Connecticut Longitudinal Study at adolescence. *Pediatrics, 104*(6), 1351–1359.

Shaywitz, S. E., & Shaywitz, B. A. (2007). What neuroscience really tells us about reading instruction: A response to Judy Willis. *Educational Leadership, 64*(5), 74–76.

Shefelbine, J., & Shiel, G. (1990). Preservice teachers' schemata for a diagnostic framework in reading. *Reading Research and Instruction, 30*(1), 30–43.

Shonkoff, J. P., & Phillips, D. A. (Eds.). (2000). *From neurons to neighborhoods: The science of early childhood development.* Washington, DC: National Academies Press.

Short, D., & Fitzsimmons, S. (2007). *Double the work: Challenges and solutions to acquiring language and academic literacy for adolescent English language learners—A report to Carnegie Corporation of New York.* Washington, DC: Alliance for Excellent Education.

Siegler, R. S., & Robinson, M. (1982). The development of numerical understandings. In H. W. Reese & L. P. Lipsitt (Eds.), *Advances in child development and behavior* (pp. 241–311). New York: Academic Press.

Simmons, D. C., & Kame'enui, E. J. (Eds.). (1998). *What reading research tells us about children with diverse learning needs: Bases and basics.* Mahwah, NJ: Erlbaum.

Skinner, C. H., Turco, T. L., Beatty, K. L., & Rasavage, C. (1989). Cover, copy, and compare: A method for increasing multiplication performance. *School Psychology Review, 18,* 412–420.

Slavin, R. E., & Lake, C. (2008). Effective programs in elementary mathematics: A best-evidence synthesis. *Review of Educational Research, 78*(3), 427–515.

Snow, M. A., & Katz, A. (2010). English language development: Foundations and implementation in kindergarten through grade five. In Center for Applied Linguistics, *Improving education for English learners: Research-based approaches* (pp. 83–127). Sacramento: California Department of Education.

Stigler, J. W., & Hiebert, J. (1999). *The teaching gap: Best ideas from the world's best teachers for improving education in the classroom.* New York: Free Press.

Storch, S., & Whitehurst, G. (2002). Oral language and code-related precursors to reading: Evidence from a longitudinal structural model. *Developmental Psychology, 38,* 934–947.

Strickland, D. S., & Barnett, S. (2003). Literacy interventions for kindergarten children considered at risk: Implications for curriculum, professional development, and parent involvement. In C. Fairbanks, J. Worthy, B. Maloch, J. V. Hoffman, & D. Schallert (Eds.), *52nd yearbook of the National Reading Conference* (pp. 104–116). Oak Creek, WI: National Reading Conference.

Swain, M. (1985). Communicative competence: Some roles of comprehensible input and comprehensible output in its development. In S. Gass & C. Madden (Eds.), *Input in second language acquisition* (pp. 235–256). New York: Newbury House.

Swanson, H. L., & Beebe-Frankenberger, M. E. (2004). The relationship between working memory and mathematical problem solving in children at risk and not at risk for serious math difficulties. *Journal of Educational Psychology, 96*, 471–491.

Swun, S. (2011). *Swun math.* Accessed at http://swunmath.com on December 22, 2011.

Teachers of English to Speakers of Other Languages. (1997). *ESL Standards for Pre-K–12 students.* Alexandria, VA: Author.

Teachers of English to Speakers of Other Languages. (2006). *PreK–12 English language proficiency standards.* Alexandria, VA: Author.

Tomlinson, C. A. (1999). *The differentiated classroom: Responding to the needs of all learners.* Alexandria, VA: Association for Supervision and Curriculum Development.

Tomlinson, C. A. (2001). *How to differentiate instruction in mixed-ability classrooms* (2nd ed.). Alexandria, VA: Association for Supervision and Curriculum Development.

Trelease, J. (1979). *The read-aloud handbook.* New York: Penguin.

U.S. Department of Education. (2004a). *Building the legacy: IDEA 2004.* Accessed at http://idea.ed.gov on May 19, 2008.

U.S. Department of Education. (2004b). *Teaching children with attention deficit hyperactivity disorder: Instructional strategies and practices.* Washington, DC: Author. Accessed at www.ed.gov/teachers/needs/speced/adhd/adhd-resource-pt2.doc on August 20, 2005.

Van de Walle, J. A. (2003). *Reform mathematics vs. the basics: Understanding the conflict and dealing with it.* Richmond: Virginia Commonwealth University.

Von Glassersfeld, E. (1995). A constructivist approach to teaching. In L. P. Steffe & J. Gale (Eds.), *Constructivism in education* (pp. 3–15). Hillsdale, NJ: Erlbaum.

Weintraub, N., & Graham, S. (2000). The contribution of gender orthographic, finger function, and visual-motor process to the prediction of handwriting status. *Occupational Therapy Journal of Research, 20*, 121–140.

Williams, T., Perry, M., Oregón, I., Brazil, N., Hakuta, K., Haertel, E., et al. (2007). *Similar English learner students, different results: Why do some schools do better?* Mountain View, CA: EdSource.

Willis, J. (2007). The gully in the "brain glitch" theory. *Educational Leadership, 64*(5), 68–73.

World-Class Instructional Design and Assessment. (n.d.). *English Language Proficiency (ELP) Standards.* Accessed at www.wida.us/standards/elp.aspx on October 23, 2011.

World-Class Instructional Design and Assessment. (2007). *English language proficiency standards prekindergarten through grade five.* Alexandria, VA: Author.

World-Class Instructional Design and Assessment. (2009). *The English language learner CAN DO booklet grades 1–2.* Alexandria, VA: Author.

Wurman, Z., & Wilson, W. S. (2012). *The Common Core math standards: Are they a step forward or backward?* Accessed at http://educationnext.org/the-common-core-math-standards/ on August 1, 2012.

Zentall, S. S. (1990). Fast-retrieval automatization and math problem solving by learning disabled, attention-disordered, and normal adolescents. *Journal of Educational Psychology, 82*(4), 856–865.

Zins, J., Weissbert, R., Wang, M., & Walberg, H. (2004). *Building academic success on social and emotional learning: What does the research say?* New York: Teachers College Press.

INDEX

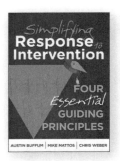

Simplifying Response to Intervention
Austin Buffum, Mike Mattos, and Chris Weber
The sequel to *Pyramid Response to Intervention* advocates that effective RTI begins by asking the right questions to create a fundamentally effective learning environment for every student. Understand why paperwork-heavy, compliance-oriented, test-score-driven approaches fail. Then learn how to create an RTI model that works.
BKF506

Pyramid of Behavior Interventions
Tom Hierck, Charlie Coleman, and Chris Weber
Students thrive when educators hold high expectations for behavior as well as academics. This book shows how to use a three-tiered pyramid of behavior supports to create a school culture and classroom climates in which learning is primed to occur.
BKF532

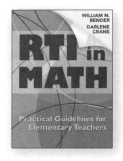

RTI in Math
William N. Bender and Darlene Crane
Explore common student difficulties in math, and see a three-tier RTI model in action. The authors provide an overview of research, detailed guidance through each stage of implementation, tools for reflection and growth, and discussion of support strategies beyond the classroom.
BKF279

Pyramid Response to Intervention
Featuring Austin Buffum, Mike Mattos, and Chris Weber
Shift to a culture of collective responsibility and ensure a path of opportunity and success for your students. Focusing on the four Cs vital to student achievement, this powerful four-part program will help you collect targeted information on each student's individual needs and guide you to build efficient team structures.
DVF057

Pyramid Response to Intervention
Austin Buffum, Mike Mattos, and Chris Weber
Accessible language and compelling stories illustrate how RTI is most effective when built on the Professional Learning Communities at Work™ process. Written by award-winning educators, this book details three tiers of interventions—from basic to intensive—and includes implementation ideas.
BKF251